Handiwork of a Glorious Creator

First Edition

Published by American Authors and Artists LLC, O'Fallon, Missouri.

American Authors and Artists LLC
1070 Bryan Road
O'Fallon MO 63366

Hebrew Concordance and other study helps provided by the Blue Letter Bible http://www.blueletterbible.org

Use of NASA photos is gratefully acknowledged and does not imply endorsement by NASA.

First Edition

2 3 4 5 6 7 8 9 0 1

Printed in the United States of America

American Authors and Artists LLC Cataloging Block

Haynes, David, 1961-
Handiwork of a Glorious Creator / David Haynes
p. cm.
ISBN #0-9822751-0-2
1. Creationism
2. Bible O.T. Genesis 1 – XI Criticism, interpretation, etc.
3. Bible and Science
231.7—dc20

Table of Contents

Figures and Tables

To Jake and all others who love the truth.

1 Foreword

Dear Friend,

I know your time is precious. There never seems to be enough time to say the things we need to say. At some point in your life you will have questions about life in general.

Scientific findings are generally considered provable as "true," and yet the Bible is generally regarded as "true." If both are true, one would expect them to agree with each other. While many say the two disagree, I find that there is remarkable agreement between the two—it all depends on one's point of view. The evidence surrounding the origin of man is considerable—as is the controversy. One can either ignore the evidence or attempt to come to terms with it.

This book attempts to reconcile scientific findings with Biblical teaching. While this is one of the most significant contemporary issues on today's academic landscape, the book doesn't merely address this single topic. In addition to developing a conceptual framework for understanding the origins of mankind, the book also endeavors to address the "who," "what," "when," "where," "why," and "how" of man's existence. I trust you will find this integrated framework useful in your journey, and the book to be an important addition to your library.

Since I enjoy a good question nearly as much as a good answer, I've presented my findings in a question/answer format. I hope you find the information helpful. In order to save you time, yet still provide the (sometimes) necessary background material, you'll find that I have organized the background material under subheadings.

Let’s start with the first question…

2 Where are we?

From a subjective reality viewpoint, about all I can tell you is that we are "here."

God gave us "reality."

None of us asked to be here, but we (billions of us) are here nonetheless. Early accounts[1] indicate that the planet was reportedly called הָאָרֶץ ("eretz")[2] by its Maker.

To say precisely where we are is a difficult thing. We need to introduce a fixed point of reference—ideally an absolute point of reference that doesn't move in space. But this isn't very easy to do. For most purposes, it's convenient to use the planet as a reference. It's been carefully mapped and devices have been built to determine one's latitude, longitude, and altitude within this mapping system. Moving beyond the planet causes us to lose this point of reference. If you were to orbit the Earth, you would find that it would not be a smooth orbit. Your altitude would go up and down as you passed over features on the planet that had more or less gravitational pull. The planet also orbits the Sun—but not at a consistent distance. Furthermore, the entire solar system is very dynamic as it moves through the Milky Way. Astronomers find that in space there are essentially rivers of matter flowing, galaxies colliding, stars and solar systems being born. On top of all of this, the very fabric of space is apparently expanding. To describe where we are

[1] The Bible, Genesis Chapter 1
[2] From this we get "Earth."

with respect to an absolute point in space isn't possible, but suffice it to say that we are here.[3]

2.1 Frame of reference

By now I'm sure you've found that life itself is in motion. You find yourself in this world, gradually getting older, perhaps wondering about life, curious about the past, and thinking about the future.

Much like the absolute and relative positioning systems (discussed above), we need an objective frame of reference in order to discuss reality.

Our own experience is by definition "subjective." So that we do not all say that "that's your truth but not mine," or "that is your reality, but I live in a different one," we all appeal to commonly known external authorities in order to make our point. The language you are reading has words that have a commonly understood definition. Much like the way people appeal to the dictionary as the authority on language, people also appeal to science as the ultimate authority with respect to reality. Others appeal to the Bible as the ultimate authority. The only true absolute authority with regard to reality would have to be someone who exists outside of the space-time continuum—someone unaffected by the ongoing changes in matter and space. This individual we know as "God," and the objective reality He communicates to us by His word (written or spoken).

2.2 Reality

"Here" has to be real for someone. It's impossible for everything to be an illusion for everybody. For there to be

[3] This in itself is an important point, because some would insist that we are not here!

an illusion, there must be someone who is suffering the illusion. There must be existence. Since you are thinking thoughts and having experiences, you must be real. The French philosopher René Descartes expressed it well: "Cogito ergo sum"—"I think, therefore I am." When you dream, when you are awake, when you fantasize, when you think clearly, you are real. Every experience you have might not be real, but they are seated in reality as a common frame of reference. God gave us "reality" as a common frame of reference. Without it, we would not have a framework with which to conceptualize things that were not real. Imagination is a wonderful thing. We all use it to speak in abstract terms about common reality—to communicate. I hope you find this book to be a useful communication, and enjoy it to the fullest.

"I think therefore I am" — Descartes

3 What are we?

3.1 The nature of man

3.1.1 Background: Why the fervent argument?

3.1.1.1 The agenda of some believers

The concern that many believers[4] have is that a natural explanation of the origin of man will somehow affect the veracity of the Genesis account. If God didn't make man, then man holds no logical accountability to God. The account of the fall of man also becomes suspect. The promise given to Eve that one of her seed would crush the serpent (which according to the Bible was ultimately fulfilled in Christ) becomes unnecessary. Believers will frequently appeal to the Bible as their authority, and will therefore seek to protect their interpretation of it.

3.1.1.2 The agenda of some scientists

Most scientists enjoy nature and are inspired by it just as nonscientists are. Some scientists would say that all they want is the truth. They would like science to be given a chance to run its course. It may support one's interpretation of the scripture. It may repudiate it. The scientific method presupposes that natural causes can explain phenomenon in nature.[5] This doesn't mean that science can explain the origin of the universe, but it should be given a chance to try. Science can hypothesize that the universe had a natural origin, but that doesn't mean that the hypothesis will be proven valid.

---

[4] Jews and Christians, but especially evangelicals.

[5] After all, when you go to boil water, you don't assume a miracle is required, but that the application of a sufficient quantity of heat will produce the desired results.

Scientists, being human beings, often carry hidden agendas of their own. For some individuals, the less responsible "god" is for the universe, the better. To them, freedom from god's authority is a fringe benefit. Other individuals take a different view and freely accept scientific teaching along side religious teaching.

3.1.1.3 My agenda

I believe there are far too much mud-slinging, too much dogma (on both sides of the issue) and too much debate. The truth can't be decided based on the outcome of a debate or by a public opinion poll. The truth is what it is. Hopefully this book will provide you with a better understanding of the two sides, and to offer a reconciliatory model of understanding between the two views. You will be challenged in life to reject your faith in one or the other.

3.1.2 How is man different from animals?

When the Bible says that "God breathed life into Adam, and he became a living being" it is primarily referring to spiritual life.[6] Likewise, when the Bible warns that the day Adam (or Eve) eat from the forbidden tree, that they will surely die, it is referring to spiritual death.[7]
Only man is spiritually alive in this way, for while God "made" the plants and animals, he "formed" man and "breathed into him the breath of life." The distinction doesn't stop there. As I read the Bible[8] I see where God

---

[6] Of course, it also implies physical "life" and "breath" as we know it. When God refers to "life" and "death," it's usually in a spiritual context with a view to the long-term ultimate reality of our existence. Meanwhile, while we refer to "life" and "death," it is usually cast in terms of our physical existence.
[7] After all, the Bible describes that Adam went on to live hundreds of years (physically) after his fall from grace.
[8] Genesis 1:27.

made plants to reproduce after their kind, animals reproduce after their kind, and if you read between the lines, God has reproduced (in a spiritual sense) after His kind. We are His offspring. God is the Father of life and of our spirit(s).

Finally we read in the Bible another distinguishing characteristic of man, that he has an elevated sense of the difference between right and wrong. All humans[9] have a sense of morality. While Adam and Eve knew it was wrong to eat from the tree of knowledge of good and evil, they were not able to judge this for themselves. They had to be told.[10] They knew that eating from the tree was wrong because it is one of the ground rules that God gave Adam. In the midst of this innocence, they had fellowship with God. Having eaten from the tree, Adam and Eve could now make the distinction between good and evil for themselves. They didn't have to rely on what they were told, they could judge for themselves between right and wrong.[11] It is arguable whether this benefited man at all. On one hand they gained a new ability they didn't have before, but on the other hand they broke fellowship with their Creator and lost more than they ever imagined.

[9] Infants generally have to be told what is right and wrong, and develop a sense of right and wrong as they mature.
[10] See Genesis 2:16-17 and Genesis 3:11.
[11] Animals on the other hand have no such awareness.

3.1.2.1 Why was it a sin for Adam and Eve to eat from the tree of knowledge of good and evil?

The Bible says[12] that "to whom much is given, much is required." With man in a state of innocence, he could not be charged with crimes of which he was unaware. But for him to know what is right, and not do it, it is sin.[13] It was just a matter of time before man (being the selfish creature he is) would do something he knew to be wrong. Adam and Eve knew that this particular act was a sin, and they committed it anyway—going against their conscience. Such an act puts man in opposition with God's law, God's will, and therefore in opposition with God Himself. One cannot knowingly commit an act of defiance against God and still be in harmony with Him.

In breaking their trust relationship with God, they lost more than their fellowship with Him. They lost a great opportunity. They could now never know what wonderful things God might have done for them in this life and in the life to come.[14] They could never know what things they (and their offspring) also might achieve in a state where they knew peace, health, long life, and God Himself.

3.1.2.1.1 Why did God include this tree in the garden?

God is exceedingly wise in so many ways. Over time, I hope we can all learn to trust Him. Some who don't quite appreciate the wisdom of His actions may accuse Him of wrong doing—of setting up man for failure. But we have to remember that this story isn't about man—the creation account is a story of something God has done. God set out

---

[12] Luke 12:48 KJV

[13] James 4:17

[14] If they were found worthy, God would have surely given them more strength, more ability, and more knowledge. I would think that this would include granting them the innate knowledge of good and evil.

to create godly offspring. To be godly offspring, man would have to have the ability to make freewill decisions (like God does).

God sometimes observes man and tests him. He set up a particularly interesting test for this couple. Adam and Eve were both gardeners. He set up a test for them which was something related to their line of work, something they understood quite well, and something easily accessible. He also had to have a contingency plan—what would happen if man were to fail the test? If they used their free will in opposition to God, could the outcome somehow drive man back to God? This test demonstrates both the brilliance and the heart of God. If man were to never fall, he would continue to walk in fellowship with God. Man would continue to learn to know what God likes and dislikes by spending time with Him in the Garden. If on the other hand, man lost that relationship with God, would there be a way for him to make better informed decisions? Would there be a way to make him less dependent on God for information? The tree holds the answer. Giving man a heightened knowledge of good and evil will bring out the character of man. If Adam and Eve did produce children, then even their offspring could have this ability and their true character could be tested by their very surroundings. If man uses his power of choice in opposition to God, he may enjoy it and become a total reprobate (and of course be judged for it). If on the other hand, man might be similarly offended by sin.[15] Perhaps such a man would call on God and turn to Him. Fortunately there is a Redeemer who can restore the relationship between God and man. He gives man hope, and a future.

[15] More on this subject in the chapter on knowing God.

You will be faced with challenges in your own life. Some questions that you'll have to consider are:

- "Is man being judged based on his own merits?"
- "Do 'good people' go to Heaven?"
- "What about the mistakes I've made in my life?"
- "Can a person change, and if so, how would God judge such a person?"

There is more on this subject in later chapters.

3.1.3 How is man different from Artificial Intelligence?

There are those who postulate that men are no different than animals, and that all such creatures are merely organic machines. Furthermore, with ongoing advances in Artificial Intelligence (AI) and computing technology it may one day be possible to "upload" patterns of human conscience into a machine. It may one day be possible to map the neural network of a particular human brain, and build a machine of sufficient scale to process the brain's computational load, and even allow this machine to interact with the environment in a robot body. This doesn't however create something equivalent to "man." Man has a spiritual dimension to him as well as physical. Man is unique on the planet in that he exists in both realms, at the same time. This puts him in an ideal position to serve as the ruler on Earth, under God and over the plant and animal kingdoms.

4 How did we get here?

4.1 Where did we come from?

In life you will find that some things are temporary, some things are "permanent," and some are eternal. We live two lives: a physical one, and a spiritual one. We know that individually we suddenly appear on the Earth—the offspring of our parents. Our lives have a sudden beginning in the physical world, but our origin in the spiritual dimension is harder to explain. The Bible says[16] that everything in this physical realm had its origins in the spiritual realm. Many of us believe that God is the Father of all things spiritual (including us) as well as all things physical (including us once again). We should not be surprised regarding the lack of *physical* evidence concerning our *spiritual* origins. However, both the Bible, and the physical evidence around us found in nature speak volumes regarding our physical origin.[17] Just as you had a rather sudden arrival into this physical realm (with your birth some years ago), the universe also had a rather sudden appearance (many billions of years ago). Both science and the Bible teach that all material things had a sudden beginning. Just as we are not born mature, the universe was not born mature either. The universe went through a stage of puberty, and is now somewhere near the middle of its lifespan.

We live two lives: a physical one and a spiritual one.

[16] Hebrews 11:3

[17] And in a similar way, the balance of this chapter will speak volumes regarding our physical origin and very little detail with regard to our spiritual origin.

4.2 The origin of all physical things

4.2.1 Background: The scientific view.

Science has made some marvelous advances in the last few decades. The current conclusion is that the origin sequence goes like this:

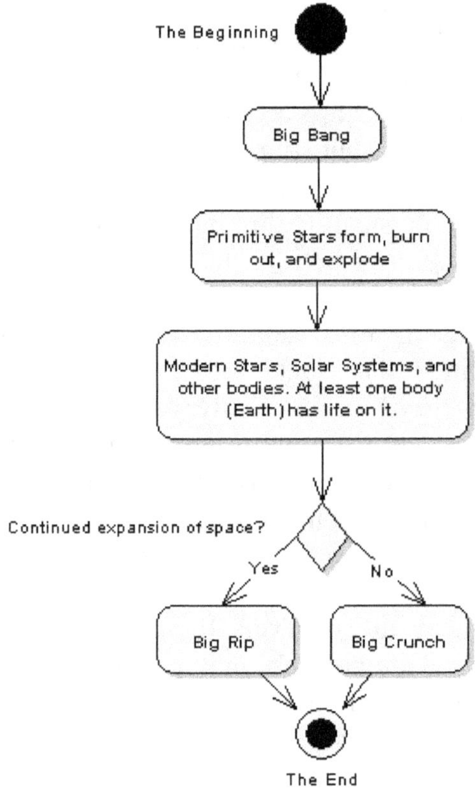

Figure 1—A brief sequence of time from Beginning to End

The current understanding of the origin of the universe is that it had a sudden beginning. Evidence is found in the echo of the big bang, the background microwave energy, the "red-shift" seen in every star, and the expansion of the universe. It is believed that the universe had a sudden beginning 13.7 billion years ago. "When the big bang occurred, matter, energy, space, and time were all formed."[18] The formation of the universe started with the formation of hot elementary subatomic particles. After 380,000 years, the matter in the universe cooled off enough to "become transparent." Elements formed and photons were able to travel. The early elements were all lightweight elements. They coalesced into primitive stars. The early primitive stars burned out early, and in their short lives produced the heavier elements. With the heavier elements available, stellar nurseries were formed. With the heavier elements available planets, stars, solar systems, and other objects are birthed. One such stellar nursery, (a molecular cloud), 200 light years[19] across came to form our solar system some 4 billion years ago. While the nebular theory is widely accepted as the explanation for the formation of solar systems, the cause of the big bang is unknown. Eventually of course, life is found on this planet. Plant life existed first, followed by life in the oceans, birds, and eventually life on land. The cause of the life and its upward progression hasn't been proven. While the theory of evolution remains the mainstay of many official government and educational systems to explain the origin of all life, many find difficulties with the theory., The theory however remains the favorite of many. A satisfactory alternative explanation that relies solely on natural (material) causation has not been found.

When the big bang occurred, matter, energy, space, and time were all formed.

[18] *Astronomy Magazine*, "The 50 Greatest Mysteries," 2007.
[19] A "light year" is the distance light will travel in one year (approximately 5.8 trillion miles).

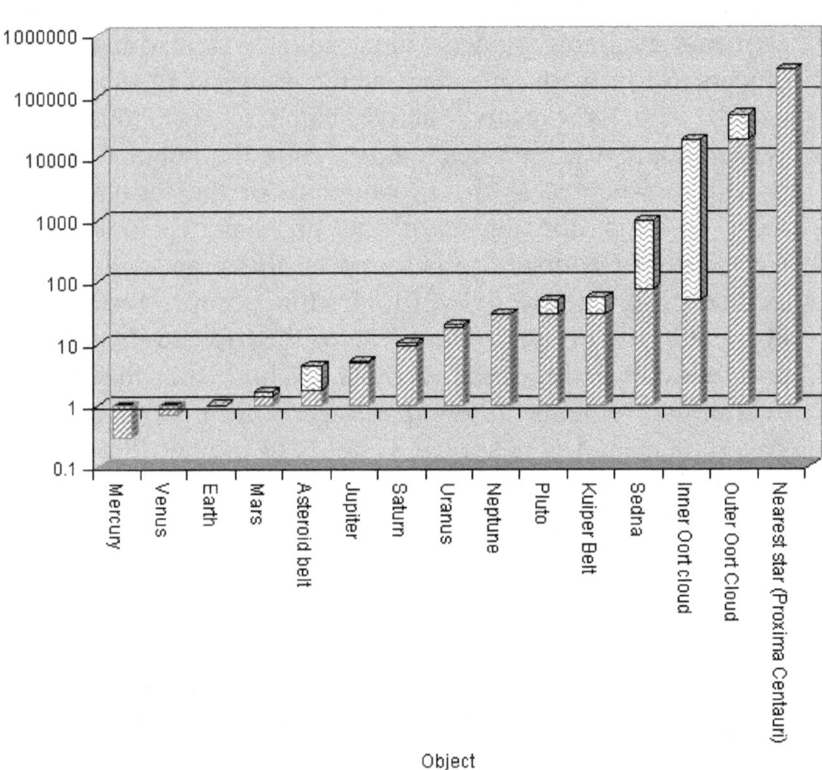

Figure 2—Distance of objects from the Sun in AU.[20]

[20] The distance from the Sun to the Earth is one astronomical unit (AU).

Object	Distance from the Sun
Nearest star (Proxima Centauri)	4.2 light years (268,000 AU)
Nearby galaxy Andromeda	2.5 million light years
Range of most power telescopes today	At least 12 billion light years in all directions

Table 1—Distance to a few distant landmarks

Our solar system contains numerous objects beyond Neptune and Pluto—the most notable being known collectively as the "Kuiper Belt" and the "Oort Cloud."

The Kuiper belt is a collection of objects in the same plane as the planets, and includes Pluto.[21] It is thought to consist of approximately 70,000 objects.

The Oort cloud is a theorized collection of comets which form a sphere around the Sun. The cloud is thought to contain trillions of objects, and range in distance from 50 to 50,000 AU from the Sun.

Our solar system has neighboring solar systems. Collectively they form a galaxy known as the Milky Way.

The size of our galaxy is amazing. It takes light approximately 180,000 light years to travel its diameter. The age of the Milky Way is thought to be nearly as old as that of the universe itself.

Every galaxy contains a collection of stars, most of which are believed to contain orbiting planets.

[21] The discovery of the Kuiper belt is one of the reasons Pluto was recently demoted from a "planet" to a "planetoid."

Scientists using the Hubble and Keck telescopes have found the most distant visible object to be emitting light from a light source when the universe was very young—only 750 million years old.

By using a wide variety of methods, it becomes quite clear that the universe had a sudden beginning, and is now 13.7 billion years old. Science can't explain what precipitated the start of the universe, or the start of life on this planet. This doesn't stop scientists from posturing theories to answer these questions.

Figure 3—Our Moon (NASA)

4.2.2 Background: The Biblical view.

The Lord declares through the prophet Isaiah:

> *It is I who made the earth and created mankind upon it.*
> *My own hands stretched out the heavens;*
> *I marshaled their starry hosts (Isaiah 45:12).*

The creation account, as recorded by Moses, states that "*In the beginning God created the heavens and the Earth.*"

4.2.2.1 Day 1—"Let there be light…"

> *…Now the earth was formless and empty, darkness was over the surface of the deep, and the Spirit of God was hovering over the waters. And God said "Let there be light, and there was light." God saw that the light was good, and he separated the light from the darkness. God called the light "day," and the darkness he called "night." And there was evening, and there was morning—the first day (Genesis 1:1-5).*

4.2.2.2 Day 2—"Let there be an expanse…"

> *And God said, "let there be an expanse between the waters to separate water from water." So God made the expanse and separated the water under the expanse from the water above it. And it was so. God called the expanse "sky." And there was evening, and there was morning—the second day (Genesis 1:6-8).*

4.2.2.3 Day 3—"Let dry ground appear…"

> *And God said, "Let the water under the sky be gathered to one place, and let dry ground appear." And it was so. God called the dry ground "land," and the gathered waters he called "seas." And God saw that it was good.*
> *Then God said, "Let the land produce vegetation: seed-bearing plants and trees on the land that bear fruit with*

seed in it, according to their various kinds." And it was so. The land produced vegetations: plants bearing seed according to their kinds and trees bearing fruit with seed in it according to their kinds. And God saw that it was good. And there was evening and there was morning—the third day (Genesis 1:9-13).

4.2.2.4 Day 4—"Let there be lights in the sky..."

And God said, "Let there be lights in the expanse of the sky to separate the day from the night, and let them serve as signs to mark seasons and days and years, and let them be lights in the expanse of the sky to give light on the earth." And it was so. God made two great lights—the greater light to govern the day and the lesser light to govern the night. He also made the stars. God set them in the expanse of the sky to give light on the earth, to govern the day and the night, and to separate light from darkness. And God saw that it was good. And there was evening, and there was morning—the fourth day (Genesis 1:14-19).

4.2.2.5 Day 5—"Let the water teem with living creatures..."

And God said, "Let the water teem with living creatures, and let birds fly above the earth across the expanse of the sky." So God created the great creatures of the sea and every living and moving thing with which the water teems, according to their kinds, and every winged bird according to its kind. And God saw that it was good. God blessed them and said, "Be fruitful and increase in number and fill the water in the seas, and let the birds increase on the earth." And there was evening, and there was morning—the fifth day (Genesis 1:20-23).

4.2.2.6 Day 6—"Let the land produce living creatures..."

And God said, "Let the land produce living creatures according to their kinds: livestock, creatures that move along the ground, and wild animals, each according to its kind." And it was so. God made the wild animals according to their kinds, the livestock according to their kinds, and all the creatures that move along the ground according to their kinds. And God saw that it was good.

Then God said, "Let us make man in our image, in our likeness, and let them rule over the fish of the sea and the birds of the air, over the livestock, over all the earth, and over all the creatures that move along the ground."

So God created man in his own image, in the image of God he created him; male and female he created them. ... God saw all that he had made, and it was very good. And there was evening, and there was morning—the sixth day (Genesis 1:24-31).

4.2.2.7 Day 7—"Finished"

Thus the heavens and the earth were completed in all their vast array.

By the seventh day God had finished the work he had been doing; so on the seventh day he rested from all his work. And God blessed the seventh day and made it holy, because on it he rested from all the work of creating he had done (Genesis 2:1-3).

4.2.2.8 Structure of the Creation Week

Biblical commentators have noted that there is a structure to the days of the creation week.

Day 1 Light	**Day 2** "Sky" to separate "waters" above the sky, from "waters" below.	**Day 3** Separate sea from dry land. Plant life.
Day 4 Sun and moon	**Day 5** Sea-creatures (e.g. Fish) and Birds	**Day 6** Land animals and man

Table 2—Structure of the creation week

On later days, God made things to rule over the things made on prior days. In Table 2, you can see the correspondence between Day 4 and Day 1, Day 5 and Day 2, Day 6 and Day 3. Man, made at the end of Day 6, is ultimately given dominion over the Earth.

From all of this, we can derive a more sophisticated view of rulership (see Figure 4).

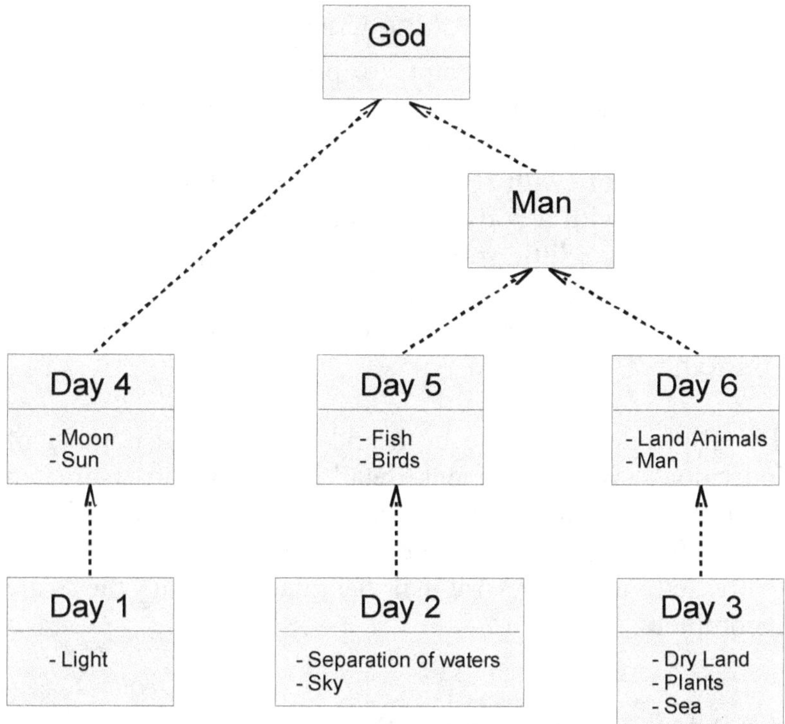

Figure 4—Hierarchical relationships (dependencies) described in Genesis 1

4.2.2.9 The Length of a "day"

The length of a "day" is a key point for consideration. This has been a stumbling point for many interpreters of the creation narrative.

The Hebrew word יום ("yowm") is frequently translated "day" in this passage, but in other places has been used to mean or translated as a "general period of time," a "lifetime," a "year," "today," "yesterday," and "tomorrow."

The way the word "day" is interpreted will govern the way the creation account is interpreted. A misleading interpretation will result in awkward constructs which are difficult to defend.

4.2.2.10 The Age of the Universe

The Bible doesn't attempt to provide an age for the universe in the creation account. Many view the narrative as merely background information to provide a context for God's dealing with His people. For Him to have a relationship with a body of people, it would be helpful for them to know a little something about the past history. For them to follow laws provided by Moses, it would be helpful for them to know that the laws flowed down from God Himself.

The Bible describes the birth and lineage of a number of individuals with sufficient detail to allow an estimated minimum age for the human race. Most place this estimate at 6,000 years. The lineages can be considered true as expressed in their original language,[22] but they are incomplete.[23]

4.2.2.11 Background: Numerous views on the creation account

4.3 My Views

It's impossible to talk about the data without at some point injecting some framework in which to interpret the data. This chapter offers one possible framework.

---

[22] In the original language, to say that someone is someone else's "son" could also be taken to mean "grandson," etc.

[23] Many consider the list to be a "Who's Who" list of patriarchs, and not an exhaustive accounting of every family member. It only takes one gap to introduce a considerable period of time.

The creation account is a story about something <u>God</u> has done.

4.3.1 The Nature of God

In order to understand the creation narrative, it is first helpful to discuss the nature of God.
The Bible says:

> *Hear, O Israel: The Lord our God, the Lord is one (Deuteronomy 6:4).*

The word "God" here is "Elohiym" in the original Hebrew. This word has a plural attribute which can indicate that God has a plural quality.[24] [25] [26]

The wording of the scripture is offering clues to its interpretation, and teaches the Trinity nature of God. Notice that it says:

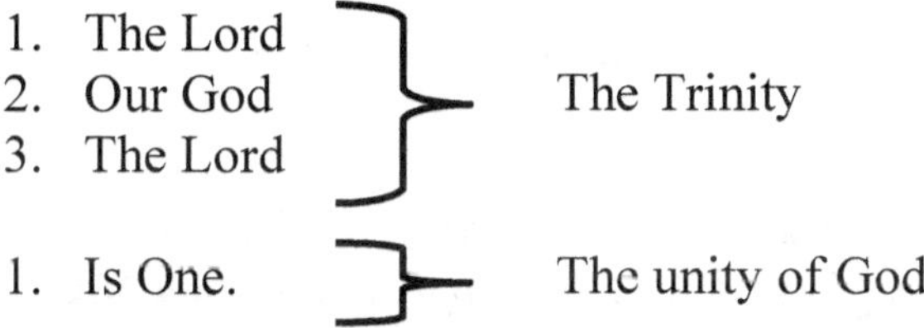

This same word for God (Elohiym) is used in the creation narrative:

---

[24] For this reason alone the Arabic "Allah," having a singular (not plural) attribute, is not an equivalent to the Hebrew "Elohiym."

[25] The singular form of God in Hebrew is "Elowahh." The text uses the plural form.

[26] The word is variously used to mean "rulers," "judges," "divine ones," "angels," or "gods."

> *Then God said, "Let us make man in our image, in our likeness..." (Genesis 1:26).*

The plural word for God; as well the three terms "us," "our," and "our," indicate the involvement of the Trinity in the creation.

4.3.2 The Source of Each Day's Light

The creation account begins with "*In the beginning God....*" This is a story about something God has done. In Rev 22:13 Jesus says that He is the "*Alpha and the Omega, the beginning and the end.*" John 1:3 says that Jesus "*made all things,*" and that there isn't anything that he hasn't made. He not only makes things He can destroy them as well. We see him shining brightly as the "*Omega*" as he destroys evil:

> *And then that lawless one will be revealed, whom the Lord Jesus will overthrow with the breath of his mouth and destroy by the splendor of his coming (2nd Thessalonians 2:8-9).*

He also shines as he illuminates the city of the New Jerusalem:

> *The city does not need the Sun or the moon to shine on it, for the glory of God gives it light (Revelation 21:23).*

Perhaps we forget that Jesus had a glory that He set aside[27] when He became a man. If at the end of all things (as the "Omega") He radiates light, then why not as the "Alpha" when creating the universe? After all Jesus prayed in the Garden of Gethsemane:

[27] See Philippians 2:6-7.

> *And now, Father, glorify me in your presence with the glory I had with you before the world began (John 17:5).*

I believe the passage "*and there was darkness, and there was light*" refers to Jesus attending to an aspect of the creation. When He shows up on the scene there is light. On the 7th day, there was nothing to attend to, the work was complete. There was no cycle of dark and light. He "rested."

The source of the light therefore was God himself. The very glory of God is described subtly on each of the six workdays. This makes Him our "glorious Creator."

The source of the light was God Himself.

Each of the following statements in the creation account are references to the appearance and work of the Lord Jesus:

- *And there was evening, and there was morning—the first day (Gen1:5).*
- *And there was evening, and there was morning—the second day (Genesis 1:8).*
- *And there was evening and there was morning—the third day (Genesis 1:13).*
- *And there was evening, and there was morning—the fourth day (Genesis 1:19).*
- *And there was evening, and there was morning—the fifth day (Genesis 1:23).*
- *God saw all that he had made, and it was very good. And there was evening, and there was morning—the sixth day (Gen1:31).*

On the seventh day we don't see this light/dark cycle because God "rested."

Consider Jesus.

> *The Son is the radiance of God's glory and the exact representation of his being, sustaining all things by his powerful word. After he had provided purification for sins, he sat down at the right hand of the Majesty in heaven (Hebrews 1:3).*

He is also called the "Word."[28]

> *In the beginning was the Word, and the Word was with God, and the Word was God.*
> *He was with God in the beginning.*
> *Through him all things were made; without him nothing was made that has been made.*
> *In him was life, and that life was the light of men.*
> *The light shines in the darkness, but the darkness has not understood it.*
> *There came a man who was sent from God; his name was John.*
> *He came as a witness to testify concerning that light, so that through him all men might believe.*
> *He himself was not the light; he came only as a witness to the light.*
> *The true light that gives light to every man was coming into the world (John 1:1-10).*

John called Him the "true light." This light was present on each of the six workdays.

[28] An obvious connection exists between Jesus being active in creation, and the Genesis 1 account where "God said…and it was."

4.3.3 The Length of Each Day

He lives outside of space and time.

He is separate from His creation.

He can traverse space and time freely.

An obvious reading of the creation account is to interpret each "day" as a 24-hour day. There are problems with this approach. Not everyone on Earth knows a cycle of light and dark as being 24-hours. To those living in the artic regions a light/dark cycle lasts months. Furthermore, the rate of spin of the Earth has changed over time. The Earth is gradually slowing. Days were somewhat shorter[29] during Adam's day than during our day. A plain reading of the English version of the text proves problematic on days 1 and 2 since there was no Sun and no Earth to gauge the passage of time. Day 7 likewise could hardly be called a day by this definition since there is no record of its beginning or ending. Readers may impose a 24-hour day structure on every day in an effort to understand the text, but this adds information which is not present in the original, and is not the only way to view the passage.

---

[29] At least a few minutes shorter based on the ongoing deceleration of the Earth due to tidal forces.

Think about the beginning for a moment. The Bible says that God (who is Spirit) made everything that is seen from things that are unseen (Hebrews 11:3).

He lives outside of space and time—because He is separate from His creation—yet He can traverse space and time freely. He is not made of protons, neutrons, and electrons. He is not made of physical matter (but of "Spirit"). He is not constrained by the laws of physics because He is not made of physical matter. He is without beginning and without ending. He is the uncaused cause of the universe, and He will one day oversee its disassembly.

He is without beginning and without end.

He is the uncaused cause of the universe.

Let's remember that this is His story. He described to Moses (the author of Genesis) events that no man could have known.[30] He described the events from His perspective.

When Moses asked Him, "who should I say is sending me," The Lord said "*tell them I AM that I AM*" (Exodus 3:14). He is the eternal existing one. Again in John 8:58, the Lord

---

[30] God expressed it as a challenge to Job "*Where were you when I laid the earth's foundation? Tell me, if you understand*" *(Job 38:4).*

explains "before Abraham was, I AM." The entire concept of a "beginning" is His invention.[31]

We see in Genesis the definition of a number of fundamentals. The planet gets a name; "sky," "land," "sea," and "day" are all defined. Spiritual light[32] emanating from the creator finds a physical corollary in the photonic light that our eyes can see.

A day is defined in the text as a cycle of darkness and light.[33] As such, the length of a day must be explained in terms of the light source. Since God was the light source, a day lasted as long as our glorious Creator was at the worksite. I believe that after completion of a particular phase of construction, He would leave the worksite. His absence would result in darkness at the worksite. His return would illuminate it once again.

Since God was the light source, a day lasted as long as our glorious Creator was at the worksite.

[31] He not only exerts His lordship in the beginning of all things, He will one day exert His lordship in the ultimate disposition of all things.
[32] "True light" as it is called.
[33] This definition became the standard in Hebrew culture. A day started at sundown, lasted through the night, and through the day, up until sundown again.

For by Him were all things created, that are in heaven, and that are in earth, visible and invisible, whether [they be] thrones, or dominions, or principalities, or powers; all things were created by him, and for him; and he is before all things, and by him all things consist. (Colossians 1:16-17 KJV)

4.3.4 Interpretation principles

Here is an important principle to keep in mind when interpreting the scriptures:

Give God credit where He asks for it.

Although we might come to understand some aspects of how God accomplished some task, we should still honor Him in those areas where He asks for it. If we come to attribute some historical milestone to a gradual natural process, we should ask "who invented nature?" A believer will say that God invented nature, and give Him the glory. An atheist will say that nature (and all that we have and know) came about by accident, and that we are very lucky indeed.

We can all appreciate that gravitational attraction (which is at work between two bodies of mass) occurs everywhere, all of the time, without daily supernatural intervention. Scientists would attribute the presence of this property to nature (i.e. "it is what it is"). A believer would go on to attribute all of nature to God (i.e. as His handiwork.)

Understanding how something works might diminish some of the mystery behind it, but shouldn't diminish our appreciation for it. After all, if we come to understand that rainbows are caused by the refraction of light through water droplets suspended in the air, does it make the rainbow any less beautiful?

With this principle in mind, God would be viewed as more than the "god of the gaps." He shouldn't merely be credited for things that science can't explain. He should be credited for things He asks credit for. (This would hold true even for Day 3 where it could be argued that little if any supernatural intervention may have been required at all.)

4.3.5 Day 1

> *...Now the earth was formless and empty, darkness was over the surface of the deep, and the Spirit of God was hovering over the waters. And God said "Let there be light," and there was light. God saw that the light was good, and he separated the light from the darkness. God called the light "day," and the darkness he called "night." And there was evening, and there was morning—the first day (Genesis 1:1-5).*

The creation account states that "*In the beginning God created the heavens and the Earth.*" I believe the introduction actually covers a number of different situations:

1. The beginning of time, space, and matter
2. The birth of primitive stars
3. The formation of heavier matter
4. The formation of numerous molecular clouds, one of which marked the start of our local system
5. The coalescence of the protosun at the middle of our system
6. The formation of an "accretion disk" around the protosun

4.3.6 The Beginning

When the Bible refers to "*The Beginning*," it refers to the beginning of all things including time itself. The Bible not only describes the beginning of time and space, but also the end of all things, and the subsequent construction of a new "heaven" and a new "Earth."[34]

God spoke and things came to be.

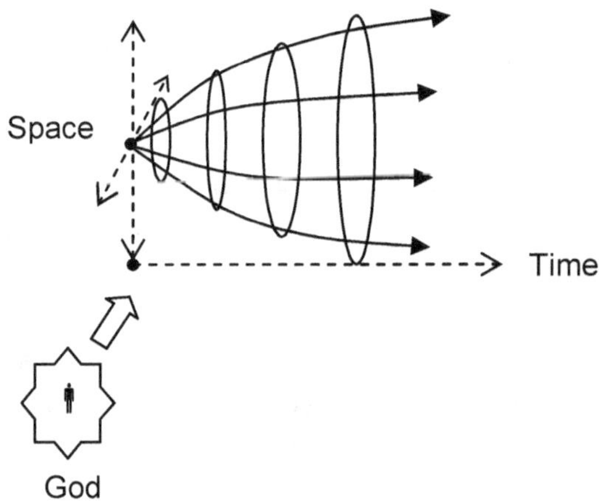

Figure 5—The glorious Creator constructing the universe

The Lord radiates glory. Whenever He enters the worksite[35] the location is illuminated. His working reveals His light and His glory. He spoke the universe into existence. He carefully engineered solutions on every level imaginable, and then built them Himself.

Isaiah 42:5 attributes credit for the existence of heavens to God:

---

[34] Revelation 21:1

[35] Perhaps, we might say, as a "carpenter" would enter a worksite.

This is what God the Lord says—
He who created the heavens and stretched them out...

In causing the Big Bang, He created physics, matter and all of its properties. He directly or indirectly formed Nebula, stars, and planets. He caused space to unfold, and matter to travel within it, all propelled away from the single pinpoint explosion of the Big Bang.

Certain activities are best accomplished in a certain order. Let's consider how a house might be built. Grading and construction of the foundation and plumbing rough-in all have to occur before the walls go up. There are certain points at which the job is done. It is reasonable to stop and take a look at the work. There are other points at which it is necessary to stop. When the cement is poured and finished, it has to be given time to set. When walls have been painted they need to be given a chance to dry. There are times, such as when a certain step has been completed, that it makes sense to pause and inspect the work. Likewise, during the construction of the universe, the Lord took time to pause and inspect His work. A number of times, He pronounced it "good." There are also times during the construction of a house, that it makes sense to do certain processes together. While one could say that a plumber installed the plumbing, there are actually numerous distinct stages. First a sewer line is entrenched under the house before it is built. The water main would probably also be tapped and routed into the home at this time. This work is done just before the foundational footing is poured—long before any walls go up. The plumbing has been started, but at this point it is far from complete. Later, after the load-bearing walls have gone up, and the interior walls have been framed, a roof is usually put on the house, and additional work occurs on the interior walls. The major services (electrical, HVAC, and of course plumbing) are routed through the floors and walls. It makes sense, as part of the construction process, to do all of this work at the same time. After this work is completed (and inspected) it will be covered with gypsum board and the next phase of construction undertaken. As the walls are completed, and the flooring is installed, the plumbing fixtures are also installed. Only when all of the pieces are in place would someone say that the house has plumbing, yet ground work for it was initiated on Day 1, and it was built over time by "the plumber." We should expect similar starts and stops as the Lord builds the universe. He is not only the architect, master carpenter, and plumber; He's the electrician, roofer, materials provider, inspector, interior decorator, property owner, and every other role.

On Day 1, we see the Lord appearing and creating the entire framework of the space-time continuum.

The Bible does not supply every detail regarding creation. It does not say if there are multiple universes similar to ours, or if there is life on other planets. We do know however that in order for there to be light, there has to be photons that travel through space. This implies there has to be "space" for the photons to travel through, and that it has to be transparent. Since travel involves motion at some speed, it also necessitates the passage of time. The light should not only have a source, but objects which can receive it.

The Bible says:

The Heavens declare the glory of God" (Psalms 19:1).

The heavens not only declare the glory of God due to their vast expanse and immense age, they declare the glory of God in the sense that they "glow." We see then in Day 1, God started the week by making something that resembles His glory, and later in Day 6, we'll see that God ended the work week by making something that represented His image (man.)

Event	Millions of Years Ago
The beginning of the universe – the "big bang"	13,700
End of initial rapid inflation and afterglow of the big bang	13,699.6
The first stars	13,300
Accelerated expansion of the universe	~9,000
Collapse of molecular cloud to form the protosun	4,592.1
Sun's Main Sequence begins	4,570

Table 3—Day 1 in terms of a scientific timeline

When the Bible says that "the Spirit of God hovered over the waters," I believe it's referring to the presence of matter prior to the production of light (from the big bang). One could say that God at this moment appears to be embracing every molecule—prior to its journey—knowing what it will become. He spoke the words "Let there be light," and the super-heated plasma cooled enough to permit photons to form and travel through space.

He spoke the desired end result.

He spoke the desired end result.

Science is saying that the universe at first was not transparent. It apparently took a while (300,000 years) after the big bang for the plasma particles to cool off and support the transmission of photons. When the Bible says that Day 1 started off in darkness, it apparently did so in multiple senses of the word.

Light, as we know, exhibits properties of both waves and particles. Photons of light have mass, have energy, occupy space, and require time to travel and exhibit their wavelike properties.

If natural "light" is considered to be the main impetus of the Day 1, then it is reasonable to think that the construction of stars (which would serve as ongoing sources of light) are an important part of the discussion. It turns out that after the big bang, most of the matter in existence at that time was thought to be hydrogen—the main source of fuel for stars.

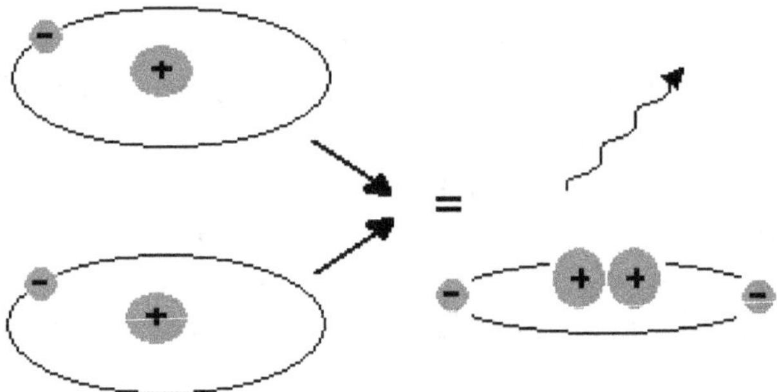

Hydrogen fusion yields Helium + energy

Figure 6—Hydrogen fusion occurs during a star's main sequence

Over time, it is believed that spent fuel from these stars formed the other elements.[36]

[36] Figure 7 shows Hydrogen (H) and Helium (He) at the top, and all of the other elements beneath them.

If primitive stars can be formed, then there is nothing to prevent other varieties of light sources—modern stars, stellar nurseries, quasars, collisions, supernovae, etc.

In saying "let there be light," it doesn't preclude other parts of the light spectrum from being present. Not only is there found in nature a rich variety in the visible spectrum from stars and molecular clouds, there exists infrared, and ultraviolet light (beyond what our eyes can see).

The statement "let there be light" also doesn't preclude extended parts of the electromagnetic spectrum from being produced either. We can expect these light sources to also produce sound (although the sound doesn't carry very well through the vacuum of space), radio waves, x-rays, and gamma rays.

The statement "let there be light" can be said to not only be one which caused light to exist, but also one that caused self-sustaining sources of light to exist.

In order for stars to be constructed, the basic forces had to be operating on the matter existing in space. The basic forces that we know about are:

- gravity
- magnetism
- strong nuclear force
- weak nuclear force

The current understanding is that certain basic elementary particles called bosons are associated with the basic forces. Elementary particles called fermions are associated with matter.

The subatomic particles build up to form atoms.

H							He
Li	Be	B	C	N	O	F	Ne
Na	Mg	Al	Si	P	S	Cl	Ar
K	Ca	Ga	Ge	As	Se	Br	Kr
Rb	Sr	In	Sn	Sb	Te	I	Xe
Cs	Ba	Tl	Pb	Bi	Po	At	Rn
Fr	Ra	Uut	Uuq	UUp	UUh	Uus	Uuo

Sc	Ti	V	Cr	Mn	Fe	Co	Ni	Cu	Zn
Y	Zr	Nb	Mo	Tc	Ru	Rh	Pd	Ag	Cd
Lu	Hf	Ta	W	Re	Os	Ir	Pt	Au	Hg
Lr	Rf	Db	Sg	Bh	Hs	Mr	Ds	Rg	Uub

La	Ce	Pr	Nd	Pm	Sm	Eu	Gd	Tb	Dy	Ho	Er	Tm	Yb
Ac	Th	Pa	U	Np	Pu	Am	Cm	Bk	Cf	Es	Fm	Md	No

Figure 7—Periodic table of the elements

It is believed that shortly after the big bang, the early matter which existed in the universe was mainly Hydrogen, some Helium, and a little Lithium. This matter clumped together to form primitive stars which "quickly" burnt out and exploded. The heavier elements in the periodic table of the elements are believed to have been formed as a result of supernova explosions. (Bear in mind that some of the heavier elements are not necessarily stable, and therefore not found in nature. They are however predicted by the model and most have been manufactured in a laboratory.)

The universe can be viewed as being a vast space containing swirling clouds of gases and debris. Explosions can push matter long distances from their point of origin. Astronomers have even noticed what could be viewed as "rivers" of matter moving through space—pulled along by gravitational forces. The matter might organize into stellar nurseries—producing new stars and continuing the Day 1 tradition of "light." The command "let there be light" was satisfied with the initial explosion of space, energy, time, and matter. But the results didn't stop there; it was fulfilled again with the formation of primitive stars. The command "let there be light" was satisfied yet again with the formation of nebula which serve as "star factories." The universe should continue to form stars for many billions of years to come.

The Bible says:

> *The Son is the radiance of God's glory and the exact representation of his being, sustaining all things by his powerful word (Hebrews 1:3).*

The glorious Creator spoke the laws of physics into existence. All physical matter is held together by these laws.

As Day 1 draws to a close, we see a universe that contains quite a bit of "star dust"—debris from activity long ago.

Our own solar system had formed a "protosun" emitting light.[37]

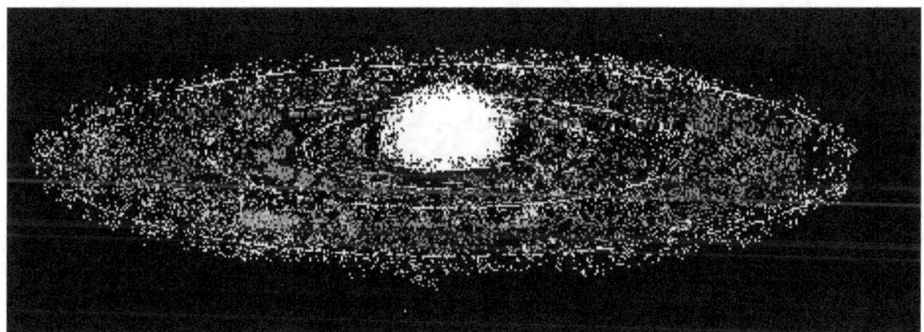

Figure 8—Protosun and accretion disk

---

[37] Scientists are making new discoveries all of the time. A fairly recent find by scientists at the University of California, San Diego, suggests that the protosun was shining early in the formation of our solar system.

The statement "let there be light" ... caused self-sustaining sources of light to exist.

The accretion disk contained ice, dust, and gas. Eventually this material ended up forming planets, asteroids, comets, and other objects.

With all of the raw materials at hand is where we find the end of Day 1 and the start of Day 2.

4.3.7 Day 2

> *And God said, "let there be an expanse between the waters to separate water from water." So God made the expanse and separated the water under the expanse from the water above it. And it was so. God called the expanse "sky" ... (Genesis 1:6-8).*

When a molecular cloud becomes cold enough, it is thought that it may lay in wait until something (such as a shock wave from a nearby nova) triggers its collapse. The collapse had already occurred on Day 1, and the protosun formed. On Day 2 we see the Lord taking care to form the Earth.

Different witnesses may describe the same event in different ways. A scientist might say that when the planet Earth was formed, a molecular cloud coalesced into a planet. The author of Genesis describes that an atmosphere formed. The two different accounts are really describing the same event.

> **A molecular cloud coalesced into a planet...an atmosphere formed. The two are ... the same.**

The molecular cloud contained material from which the sun, planets, and even comets were made. Comets are commonly referred to as "dirty snowballs" because they contain large amounts of water. The accretion disk contained large amounts of water (as well as other materials). The Genesis narrative focuses on the *space* that was made in the molecular cloud, by essentially "parting the waters" leaving a carefully portioned amount of material in the form of a planet, and the rest out in space. The Earth was given the right amount of iron to form a good core, water to form oceans, and the many other elements that we find today. This doesn't mean however that the world we know today is the same as the day it was made. Science tells us that the atmosphere was very different back then. We also know that the Moon was formed slightly after the Earth was formed, and that they share a lot of common material.

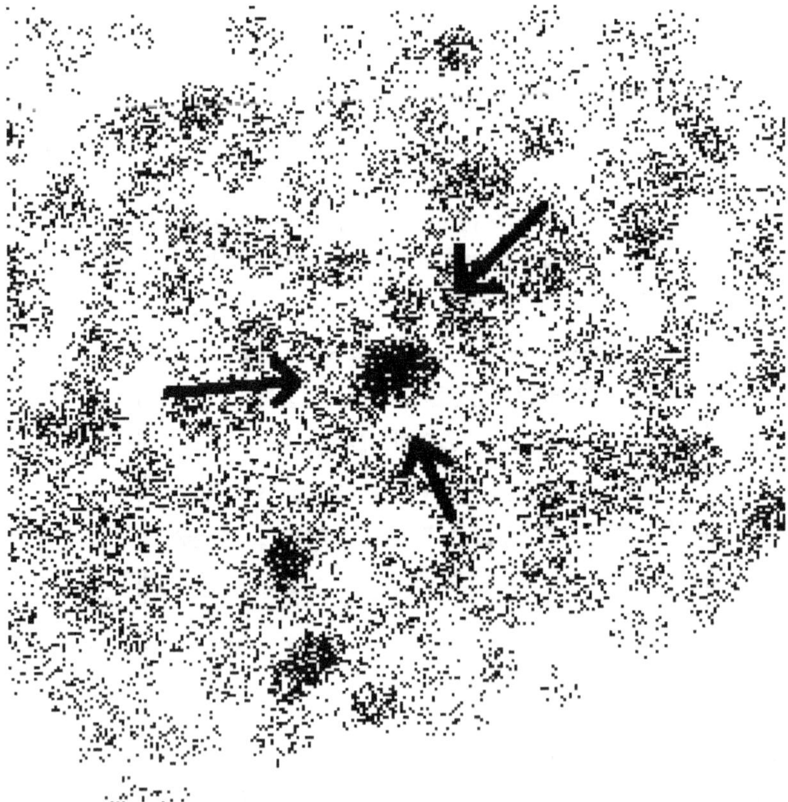

Figure 9—Molecular cloud coalesces into a sun and planets

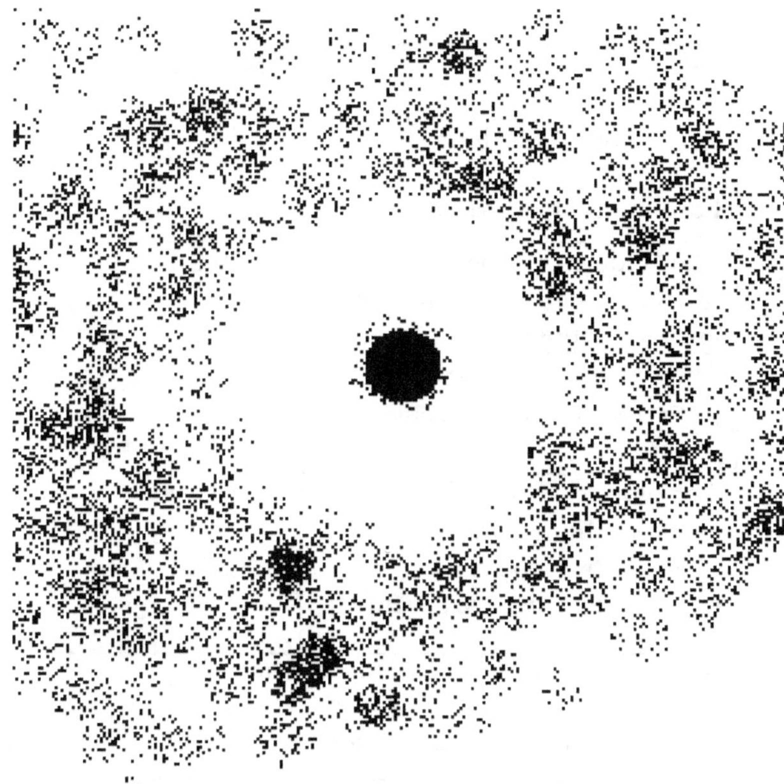

Figure 10—Coalescence creates expanse (or "sky")

The continued presence of the accretion disk around the planets would obscure the primitive sun.

Event	Millions of Years Ago
Formation of Earth	4,540
Formation of the Moon	4,527
The Hadean Eon begins with the formation of the earth and lasts for about a billion years.	4,540-3,800
The Earth was formed in the presence of large amounts of water.	
The oldest known mineral (4400 million years ago) and oldest known rocks (4100 million years ago) are formed.	

Table 4—Day 2, in terms of a scientific timeline

The Hadean Eon is named in honor of "Hades." The Earth during this time was very hot – with most rocks melting or quickly weathering away, frequent volcanic activity, earthquakes, and meteor impacts.

At the end of Day 2 we find that the Earth exists as a planet, but it is still very inhospitable. It needs a lot of work in order for it to become habitable.

4.3.8 Day 3

> *And God said, "Let the water under the sky be gathered to one place, and let dry ground appear." ...*
> *Then God said, "Let the land produce vegetation: seed-bearing plants and trees on the land that bear fruit with seed in it, according to their various kinds." And it was so. The land produced vegetations: plants bearing seed according to their kinds and trees bearing fruit with seed in it according to their kinds ... (Genesis 1:9-13).*

We see throughout the creation account where God spoke, and things happened.

Much like a baseball pitcher that, through his skill, can cause the ball to slide in or out, curve up or down, long after the ball leaves his hands; God spoke a word, and it went out having the effect He intended.

His word will not return to Him empty.

The Lord says that His word will not return to Him empty,

> *but will accomplish what I desire and achieve the purpose for which I sent it* (Isaiah 55:11).

We've already seen this principle at work. The laws of physics established during Day 1, are still at work during Day 2, and every day thereafter. They have the ongoing effect He intended. God said "light be" and "light was" again and again and again. A similar thing happens with plant life. A word is set in motion during Day 3, and continues working until it accomplishes what He intended.

The next step for the formation of the Earth was for large bodies of water to form. While much of this can be considered to be the result of the laws of nature God established on Day 1, and the amount of water He allocated to the Earth on Day 2, the work on Day 3 doesn't stop there. It contains the first signs of life! The Lord starts the "terraforming" process as early as possible. Plants of course are crucial for producing oxygen and changing the atmosphere. The Lord creates plant life on Day 3—before the direct light of the Sun is revealed. He made plants that could tolerate the shade—using light which didn't "rule" the Day. (See Day 4 below for more discussion.)

Event	Millions of Years Ago	Eon
Lots of geologic activity	3,800-2,500	Archaean
No large continents		
Proto-continents come and go		
Sun was dim		
No free oxygen		

Table 5—Day 3 in terms of a scientific timeline

The Archaean eon saw the start of cyanobacteria including oxygen producing varieties (such as plankton). Science says that eventually, many millions of years later, during the Proterozoic eon (Day 4), the plants improved, but most of the action was in the oceans. During the start of the Phanerozoic eon (Day 5) the Earth experienced a greenhouse phase. Plants flourished on the land including seeded plants. According to our understanding of the fossil record, trees appeared at the start of the Day 6. The land was covered with great plants, and great coal beds developed. They appeared just in time to support the land animals which were created as the subject of Day 6. So while the creation of plants was fulfilled on Day 3, it was fulfilled again and again with new species being introduced as they were needed on successive days.[38]

How easy it is, with our familiar way of thinking, to limit God. A God who lives outside of space and time could easily travel through the space-time continuum, and do His work. The one called the "Word" could begin His journey at this point in the continuum to make the simplest of plants. He could continue on his campaign to other points in the continuum to make more advanced species of plants at the point in time where they are needed. He could ultimately finish His efforts with the seed bearing plants described in the narrative. This is His Word going forth to accomplish His will. The other members of the godhead were also active in the creation. We've already seen where the Holy Spirit was involved in the creation. God is capable of being everywhere at the same time. Since He is also eternal, this amounts to His pervasive presence throughout creation as He desires.

So, at the end of Archaean eon, we find a relatively stable planet in place, with the first life (and as far as we know, the only life in the universe) operating on planet Earth. The planet still had a long way to go before it would become habitable by more advanced life forms.

[38] While it might be possible that seed bearing plants and trees existed on land long before land animals, fossils haven't been found to support such a claim.

4.3.9 Day 4

> *And God said, "Let there be lights in the expanse of the sky to separate the day from the night, and let them serve as signs to mark seasons and days and years, and let them be lights in the expanse of the sky to give light on the earth." And it was so. God made two great lights—the greater light to govern the day and the lesser light to govern the night. He also made the stars. God set them in the expanse of the sky to give light on the earth, to govern the day and the night, and to separate light from darkness ... (Genesis 1:14-19).*

You'll recall that on Day 1 God created space, time, and matter. The universe was initially opaque. The work to clear away the fog occurred long ago. It is believed that the same stars that created light also served to clear away the interstellar fog. The creation of the heavier elements may have also coincided with the creation of dark matter. We really do not understand what dark matter is, or where it came from, but we do know that dark matter appears to be contributing to the accelerated expansion of the universe. Could this also contribute to keeping the universe observable? Perhaps in time, when we come to understand it better, we'll know the answer.

From Day 2, since the formation of the Earth, the Sun was obscured by debris in the accretion disk (in space itself between the Earth and the Sun), as well as debris in the upper atmosphere (of the Earth).

Over time a number of things happened:

1. The solar output of the Sun increased.
2. The debris in the accretion disk settled onto planets, asteroids, or was pushed away by the solar wind (some of which become comet material.)
3. The dust in the atmosphere cleared.

These all contributed to allow the Sun to now serve as a "sign" in the sky. It became a distinct object in the sky rather than an obscure light source. The moon also could be clearly seen, and in time, the stars also. These objects weren't *made* on Day 4, but they were *made to become signs*[39] (as the scripture says) to those on the Earth.

So one might say "where's the miracle?" A miracle is when God gets personally involved to change the natural order of events. Clearly on Day 1, when God created the framework for time and space—that was a miracle. Tuning the parameters to allow the universe to operate was a miracle. On Day 2 He got involved shaping the Earth. On Day 3 He got involved proportioning the continents and oceans, and initiating plant life. It seems that on Day 4, over and above any natural processes that may have occurred, He got personally involved to clean up the debris. The Carpenter who framed the universe, roughed and finished the planetary bodies, and initiated the terraforming process, spent time to clean up the debris before granting an occupancy permit for any living creatures.

The Earth is particularly well suited to sustain life:

1. The atmosphere tends to burn up any meteorites (debris) which may strike.
2. The water and air allow for interaction between plants and animals, and contains the right mixture of gases to promote life and deter fires.
3. It has a circular (not elliptical orbit) which helps prevent wild temperature fluctuations. Plus, it is not so near the Sun to get roasted nor so far that it gets too cold.
4. It contains large amounts of water—known to be necessary to support the chemical reactions necessary for active, mobile life as we know it.

---

[39] Genesis 1:14

5. The Earth is protected by an invisible magnetic shield which protects against harmful radiation.

But the Earth is also well positioned for viewing the universe:

1. The planet is not ringed with debris.
2. The gases in every level[40] of the atmosphere are transparent.
3. The circular orbit of the Earth provides a stable platform for observing seasonal events which occur in an easily predictable pattern.
4. Dust and water vapor may accumulate into clouds, but the rain serves to clear the air[41] as well as sustain life.
5. Observers are protected from the many dangers of space, but enjoy the benefits of:
    - the Sun
    - gravity
    - protection from most meteorites

Furthermore, our solar system is not:

- presently located in or near a molecular cloud
- located in or near a stellar cluster
- in the middle of its galaxy

Compare Earth to its neighboring planets: Mars and Venus.

Venus is the second planet from the Sun, while Earth is the third. Both planets are similar in size, gravity, and bulk composition. Venus has a dense atmosphere consisting primarily of carbon dioxide. The dense atmosphere (about 92 times thicker than that of Earth!) maintains very high temperatures on the surface of the planet. Venus also has a highly reflective cloud cover of sulfur dioxide and sulfuric

---

[40] Even the oceans are clear!

[41] Large optical telescopes can often see through a certain amount of cloud cover anyway.

acid which prevents direct light from reaching the surface. Why didn't the Earth, similar in size and composition, end up with a similar atmosphere? Many believe something happened to the Earth which intervened. Perhaps the formation of the moon played a part. Perhaps it was something more.

Mars is another case study. Mars is the fourth planet from the Sun. The planet is about $1/10^{th}$ the size of Earth. The atmosphere (again) is primarily carbon dioxide, but the atmospheric pressure is less than $1/100^{th}$ that of Earth's. So, while not covered with clouds of reflective gas, the thin air is often stirred up to create the largest dust storms of any planet in the solar system. Much of the light which reaches the surface is diffuse. Mars lacks a magnetic field and is unable to protect its atmosphere from the solar wind. Its surface is frequently pelted with radiation and with meteorites. Equipment we send to Mars is frequently lost. The planet is frigid and inhospitable. There are insufficient quantities of oxygen and water to freely support life as we know it. The inhospitableness ranges from bad to worse due to its elliptical orbit. While there might be certain times of the year Mars could be used as an observation post, we humans couldn't live there without spacesuits and special, hardened living quarters.

On Day 2, God created "sky" and separated the "water" from above the sky from the water below. What happened to the water above the sky? The last of the molecular cloud was dispersed on this day. The lighter gases which didn't get drawn into the Sun were either drawn to a planet or dispersed as part of the thin gas which forms the interstellar medium. The heavier materials (which didn't fall into the Sun or a planet or form an asteroid) were also pushed away on this day. These remnants of the accretion disk are thought to exist as solid objects primarily located in the Kuiper Belt, and Oort cloud. These two vast collections are so well hidden from view, that our most powerful telescopes have only recently found the Kuiper belt, and have yet to find the Oort cloud. (They're certainly not in the way of observing the stars.)

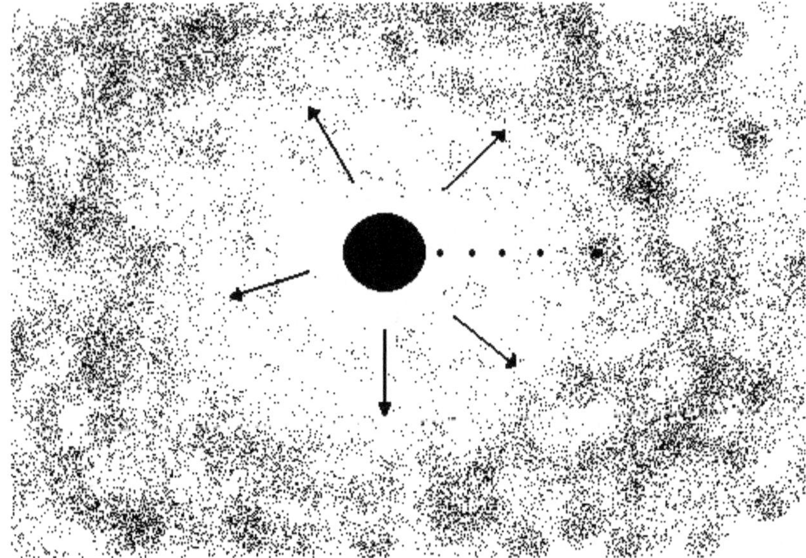

Figure 11—Solar wind pushes away dust.

The solar wind would have pushed particles away from the Sun, and eventually away from the planets. Over time the diffuse sunlight became direct sunlight. A greater distinction would be made between "day" and "night." The "day" would obviously become brighter due to direct sunlight, but the "night" would also become darker because there would be less backscatter reflecting off of the debris to reach the backside of the planet.

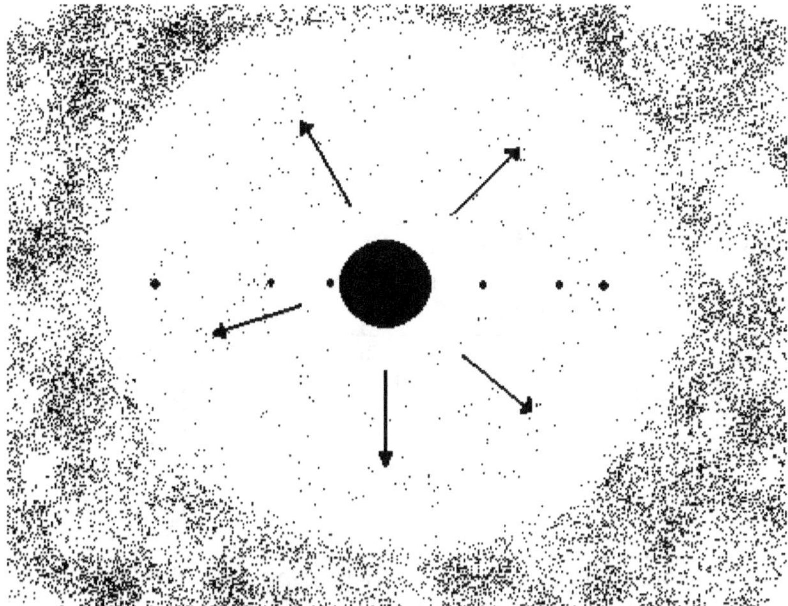

Figure 12—Sunlight eventually pushes dust beyond planets

The ultimate dissipation of the molecular cloud would reveal the (previously created) stars to viewers on Earth. The (recently discovered) Edgeworth-Kuiper belt is believed to be the remnants of the accretion disk where gravity found its balance against the solar wind, and the particles coalesced into small planetoids.[42]

Moon samples imply that the moon was formed about the same time as the Earth, about 4.5 billion years ago. Scientists believe that the moon was formed when a large (planetary sized) object struck the Earth in a glancing blow. Needless to say, such an event would have been rather

---

[42] The remaining dust was either pushed into the Ort cloud, pushed into interstellar space, pulled into a nearby gravitational body, joined with an Edgeworth-Kuiper Object (EKO), drawn into the sun, or perhaps remains as part of the dust floating about the solar system today.

catastrophic on the Earth, and would have stirred up considerable debris in space as well.

Event	**Millions of Years Ago**	**Period**	**Era**
Iron removed from oceans	2,500-2,300	Siderian	Paleo-proterozoic (Cyano-bacteria produce oxygen.)
Eukaryote cells	2,300-2,050	Rhyacian	Paleo-proterozoic
Two of the largest known impact events	2,050-1,800	Orosirian	Paleo-proterozoic
The supercontinent Columbia is formed.	1,800-1,600	Statherian	Paleo-proterozoic
Breakup of the supercontinent Columbia	1,600-1,400		Meso-proterozoic (Transition to an oxygenated atmos-phere.) Calymmian

Event	Millions of Years Ago	Period	Era
Eukaryotic red algae, oldest known sexually reproducing organism and oldest known multi-cellular organism	1,400-1,200	Ectasian	Meso-proterozoic
Land fungi thought to propagate			
Assembly of super continent Rodinia	1,200-1,000	Stenian	Meso-proterozoic
Breakup of supercontinent Rodinia	1,000-850	Tonian	Neo-proterozoic
Glaciations	850-630	Cryogenian	Neo-proterozoic
Increase in primitive land based plants			
Unusual depletion of C^{13}	635-542	Ediacaran	Neo-proterozoic

Table 6—Day 4 corresponds fairly well to the Proterozoic Eon

The creation involves nearly every work role imaginable. Thus far we've already seen some pretty amazing feats. In creating nature, God created all things related to science. In creating the stars, planets, and other artifacts, God performed amazing feats of engineering and construction, with skill and understanding that we can appreciate but scarcely comprehend. But on Day 4 we find the Lord performing a much more humble role. He's performing some "housekeeping." The space around the Sun is being swept clean. Some might say that this was purely a natural process and that God was not involved, but Who invented nature?! The geological record also shows that some serious housekeeping was being done on the planet below. The continents were being rearranged. Some major impacts occurred which required cleanup before the habitat would be suitable for keeping the kind of life forms He had in mind. While we could all perhaps live in a world that was less clean, the Bible indicates that the Lord was preparing the Earth for habitation, and preparing the skies for astronomy. Our ability to see our surroundings is so important to our lifestyle and to enjoy the freedom and authority that He's given us. A world covered in darkness could not support the complex ecosystem we enjoy today.

We might never come to fully appreciate the work done to space, the area around the Sun, and to our own atmosphere. One thing we have found however is that the changes occurring in the sky had a corresponding affect on the situation on the Earth. The increased levels of sunlight had an understandable effect on the plant and bacterial life, which in turn had an affect on the chemistry of the planet. These changes were necessary to support the creatures that would be made on Day 5.

In creating the stars, planets, and other artifacts, God performed amazing feats of engineering and construction, with skill and understanding that we can appreciate but scarcely comprehend.

4.3.10 Day 5

> *And God said, "Let the water teem with living creatures, and let birds fly above the earth across the expanse of the sky." So God created the great creatures of the sea and every living and moving thing with which the water teems, according to their kinds, and every winged bird according to its kind. And God saw that it was good. God blessed them and said, "Be fruitful and increase in number and fill the water in the seas, and let the birds increase on the earth" ... (Genesis 1:20-23).*

Science agrees with the Bible in the sense that life started in the oceans. What science can't explain is how life got started. Much like the unexplainable origin of the universe, life itself, according to the theory of evolution, started or evolved upward into ever increasing complexity. Not all scientists agree with this theory, and even many evolutionists are dissatisfied with this theory, but lack any other credible theory to replace it. The Bible of course doesn't lack in this area—teaching that God created the life in the seas and in the air.

Science agrees with the Bible... life started in the oceans.

The fossil record documents the sudden introduction of a huge variety of marine creatures—the most remarkable of which is known as the "Cambrian explosion." The fossil record shows that for long periods of time, very little happened, then, in a relatively short period of time, numerous revolutionary designs were introduced. The fossil record also shows that the majority of the designs were eliminated—sometimes by major extinction events.

Event	Millions of Years Ago	Period	Era
Multi-cellular (The Cambrian explosion)	542-488	Cambrian	Paleozoic
Two major extinction events	490-440	Ordovician	Paleozoic
Many important changes in marine life			
Continent Gowanda drifts South	443-416	Silurian	Paleozoic
Earth enters a long greenhouse phase			

Table 7—Day 5 corresponds to the start of the Phanerozoic Eon

The earliest known fossils for insects (winged creatures) appeared later in the Paleozoic era during the Devonian period. Some believe insects started earlier, but the evidence hasn't yet been found. More sophisticated (and in some cases gigantic) insects appeared in the Carboniferous and Permian periods.

While most translations use the word "birds" in Genesis 1:20, it can just as well be translated "winged creatures. The Hebrew word עוף ('owph) can be translated "flying creatures," "fowl," "insects," or "birds."

The Day 5 proclamation was fulfilled technically with the creation of the many sea creatures and winged insects, but the work didn't stop there. New species of creatures in the sea and in the air were created at different points in time throughout the remainder of the Phanerozoic eon; each kind reproducing after their kind; each radically new advanced species was designed by a glorious Creator who developed ecosystem after ecosystem time after time.

4.3.11 Light Travels Through Time

Some might say that it's inconceivable to think that God would travel through time on a campaign to do His work. Consider however the fact that with our very own eyes we are witnesses to light that has traveled great distances, through time, to reach us. When we look at the stars, the light from some has traveled years, some tens of years, some hundreds, some thousands, some millions, some billions of years. Since we are witness to this fact of nature, perhaps it will become easier to believe that the true Light would travel about to accomplish His will.

4.3.12 Day 6

> *And God said, "Let the land produce living creatures according to their kinds: livestock, creatures that move along the ground, and wild animals, each according to its kind." And it was so. God made the wild animals according to their kinds, the livestock according to their kinds, and all the creatures that move along the ground according to their kinds. ... Then God said, "Let us make man in our image, in our likeness, and let them rule over the fish of the sea and the birds of the air, over the livestock, over all the earth, and over all the creatures that move along the ground."*
> *So God created man in his own image, in the image of God he created him; male and female he created them.*

> *God blessed them and said to them, "Be fruitful and increase in number; fill the earth and subdue it. Rule over the fish of the sea and the birds of the air and over every living creature that moves on the ground." ...*
> *God saw all that he had made, and it was very good. And there was evening, and there was morning—the sixth day (Genesis 1:24-31).*

The work on Day 6 forms the culmination of the creation event. The focus of the activity transitions from the sea to the development of complex ecosystems on land. Plant life improved, and at the same time, the Lord introduced numerous new designs of land animals. On this day the Lord created all kinds of creatures that move along the ground, with numerous different designs and levels of complexity, until ultimately creating man.

4.3.13 Observations

We see throughout the creation account that "God said…and it was so." With the creation of land animals we read where God said "let the land produce living creatures…." This is a rather distant involvement by God with His creation. But when it comes to the creation of man, God gets very personal. He says "Let us make man in our image…." Genesis 2 goes on to describe the creation of man in detail, and that:

> *the Lord God formed the man from the dust of the ground and breathed into his nostrils the breath of life, and the man became a living being (Genesis 2:7).*

There is a wide variety of involvement and technique on God's part, in the way He made the universe.

- On Day 1, God "spoke" things into existence—and laws of physics were "formulated."
- On Day 6 we see God commanding the "land to bring forth" species. Some would call this

"evolution." The brilliant designs of the plants and animals speak volumes for God's involvement, but it wasn't very personal.
- We see later on Day 6 where God "formed" man from the dust of the ground. This is more personal than "speaking" something into existence, but God's personal involvement doesn't stop there. He "breathed into his nostrils the breath of life and the man became a living being."

In the original text, the same word for "breath" also means "spirit." God gave man physical life and spiritual life. In giving man spiritual life, He gave man some of the same nature that God has. It is this nature that makes Him eternal, and we as a result are likewise eternal. So while Day 3 ended with the first known life in the physical universe, Day 6 ended with the only life to uniquely span the physical and spiritual worlds.

- **Day three ended with the first known life in the physical universe.**
- **Day six ended with the only life to uniquely span the physical and spiritual worlds.**

Philosophers, poets, and scientists have long marveled at what makes man so different from the rest of creation. The Bible explains that man is truly unique because he was made in God's image. He is also unique because he was commissioned by God to rule over the other parts of creation. The Bible says that we are, in very humble circumstances, essentially "gods." The Bible describes in subsequent chapters that man initially had a relationship with our creator. The Bible describes how this relationship was broken, and on that day, man "died" spiritually. The good news however is that God "so loved the world" that He had a rescue plan in mind should it be required.[43]

[43] Be sure to read on and find the sections "Why would God even Care?" and "Why are we here?"

Event	Millions of Years Ago	Period	Era
Rhizome based plants	416-359	Devonian	Paleozoic
Insects			
Spiders			
First land animals			
First trees			
Coal beds developed	359-299	Carbon-iferous	Paleozoic
Supercontinent Pangeia formed	299-251	Permian	Paleozoic
Permian ends with the largest extinction event			
Ninety to ninety-five percent of marine species, and 70% of land organisms become extinct			
Pangeia starts to break apart	251-199	Triassic	Mesozoic
Volcanic activity and large meteorite impact occurs			
More extinctions			
More development of sea life, reptiles, and dinosaurs			
"Age of the dinosaurs"	199-150	Jurassic	Mesozoic
First birds			

Event	Millions of Years Ago	Period	Era
Chalk beds formed in Europe	145-65.5	Cretaceous	Mesozoic
Pangeia breaks up to form modern continents			
Mammals	65.5-23	Paleogene	Cenozoic
Further development of mammals and birds	23-0	Neogene	Cenozoic
Homo 1.8 mya[44]			
Homo Sapian 0.5-0.3 mya			
Homo Sapian Sapian 0.150 mya			

Table 8—Day 6 corresponds to the end of the Phanerozoic Eon

[44] Million Years Ago (MYA)

4.3.14 Day 7

> *Thus the heavens and the earth were completed in all their vast array.*
> *By the seventh day God had finished the work he had been doing; so on the seventh day he rested from all his work. And God blessed the seventh day and made it holy, because on it he rested from all the work of creating he had done (Genesis2:1-3).*

We see on Day 7 there is no cycle of evening and morning such as all of the previous days had. Many scholars conclude from this that there was no end to Day 7, and that we are still in Day 7 to this day.

What is God doing on Day 7? It would make sense that He would use the opportunity to enjoy His creation. After all if His ultimate purpose in making the universe was to make man and enjoy him, then now having made man, it's time to enjoy him! He formally sets aside this day for this purpose, but the relationship ran into trouble. God is ultimately faced with a decision (which He decided before the foundation of the world) which caused Him to do something on Day 7 which is more remarkable than any of the days before.

The Sabbath (Day 7) was meant for a time spent with family and with God. What's amazing is that God is living this during Day 7. He is spending His time enjoying His creation—especially man. Man was part of His family—being made in His image. But His offspring was in trouble. God could no longer spend time enjoying and fellowshipping with man because of his sin. During Day 7 God performed an act of restoration, restoring the relationship that brings life.[45]

---

[45] There are untold millions that have a relationship with Him. Are things going well in your relationship with the Lord? He promises that

The Sabbath rest doesn't mean God does nothing at all[46], or that His people are to do nothing at all. In fact Jesus said that He goes to prepare a place for us.[47]

This universe, as we know, is built to have three spatial dimensions (often called "width," "height," and "depth") as well the aspect of "time.[48]" But scientists have often speculated "what if the universe were built differently?" What if it only had one or two dimensions? What if it didn't have the aspect of "time?" The Bible says that one day God will reveal a new universe that He is building for us. It will be revealed at the "end of time" at a point after the current universe has been dissolved by fire. The new heaven and a new "Earth"[49] will be a system without the need for a sun, because the glory of God will provide the light to illuminate it.

> *The city does not need the sun or the moon to shine on it, for the glory of God gives it light ... (Revelation 21:23).*

4.3.14.1 The Sabbath as law

The creation account was given to Moses, as were the Ten Commandments, and a number of societal laws. The six day workweek was ordained by God. He framed His own efforts as a six "day" workweek as a teaching mechanism. He wanted people to take a day off work, not just for their own good, and to spend time with their families,[50] but to consider Him.[51]

---

if you seek Him, you will find Him. I'd like to encourage you to seek Him and develop a personal relationship with Him.

[46] Luke 6:9

[47] John 14:2

[48] Sometimes called "the fourth dimension."

[49] Revelation 21:1.

[50] See Exodus 16:29 – the miracle of manna in the wilderness.

[51] See Leviticus 23:3.

> *For in six days the Lord made the heavens and the earth, the sea, and all that is in them, but he rested on the seventh day. Therefore the Lord blessed the Sabbath day and made it holy (Exodus 20:11).*

No one[52] has seen God the Father at any time. But, people have seen God the Son (who gave the law).

> *Moses and Aaron, Nadab and Abihu, and the seventy elders of Israel went up (the mountain) and saw the God of Israel. Under his feet was something like a pavement made of sapphire, clear as the sky itself (Exodus 24:9-10).*

4.3.14.2 The Lord of the Sabbath

Although He ... rested on the Sabbath, He ... returned a seventh time...

> *One Sabbath Jesus was going through the grain fields, and his disciples began to pick some heads of grain, rub them in their hands and eat the kernels.*
> *Some of the Pharisees asked, "Why are you doing what is unlawful on the Sabbath?"*
> *Jesus answered them, "Have you never read what David did when he and his companions were hungry?*
> *He entered the house of God, and taking the consecrated bread, he ate what is lawful only for priests to eat. And he also gave some to his companions."*

---

[52] No man except Jesus the God-man (see John 6:46).

> *Then Jesus said to them, "The Son of Man is Lord of the Sabbath."*
>
> *On another Sabbath he went into the synagogue and was teaching, and a man was there whose right hand was shriveled.*
>
> *The Pharisees and the teachers of the law were looking for a reason to accuse Jesus, so they watched him closely to see if he would heal on the Sabbath.*
>
> *But Jesus knew what they were thinking and said to the man with the shriveled hand, "Get up and stand in front of everyone." So he got up and stood there.*
>
> *Then Jesus said to them, "I ask you, which is lawful on the Sabbath: to do good or to do evil, to save life or to destroy it?"*
>
> *He looked around at them all, and then said to the man, "Stretch out your hand." He did so, and his hand was completely restored (Luke 6:1-10).*

The irony occurring here is that this same God who:

- did the work of creation in six "days"
- rests on the seventh day
- developed the concept of a Sabbath rest as a law
- wrote it into the ten commandments with his own hand[53]

is ultimately accused of violating the law He established!

Jesus taught here that it was lawful to do good on the Sabbath. He had a much larger agenda, and was teaching with regard to His mission.

> *Jesus asked the Pharisees and experts in the law, "Is it lawful to heal on the Sabbath or not?"*
>
> *But they remained silent. So taking hold of the man, he healed him and sent him away.*

---

[53] Exodus 31:18

> *Then he asked them, "If one of you has a son or an ox that falls into a well on the Sabbath day, will you not immediately pull him out?" (Luke 14:3-5).*

There was a problem of cosmic proportions that God came to solve. Jesus said:

> *This is eternal life ... to know ... God (John 17:3).*

Spiritual death had befallen mankind. God was faced with either destroying man (in order to contain the problem) or stepping in personally to lift man out of the pit into which he had fallen. Before the foundation of the world,[54] God opted to save man rather than destroy him.

Did you know that the penalty for violating the Sabbath law was death? Why was that? It's because the Sabbath represents the fellowship with God and man, and a person who doesn't have this fellowship is "dead." A person who has this fellowship is "alive" and enjoys God's rest.[55] I pray you find this relationship and know His rest and thus find life.

4.3.15 Difficulties with the Theory of Evolution

The theory assumes that life would somehow evolve from simpler life forms to more complex life forms. The natural process which has the best chance of explaining this is to rely on random genetic mutation to introduce variety, and also rely on predators and similar mechanisms to remove certain creatures with particular traits from the population. While theses processes no doubt do play a role in shaping the make-up of the population, it has been a matter of

[54] 1 Peter 1:20
[55] See also Hebrews 4:1-11

intense debate as to the sufficiency of these processes to explain the entire spectrum of life seen in the fossil record.

4.3.15.1 Information Content

This theory of evolution assumes that a simple cell such as a plant could evolve to become a bacteria, virus, or multi-celled animal. A cursory study of these life forms however shows just how dissimilar they are. One could easily take the view that these are completely separate designs.

The amount of information in a strand of human DNA is staggering. Even the simplest life-forms are amazingly complex. Can a gradual random process to generate variety coupled with natural section to eliminate certain "undesirable" members lead to entirely new species?

An analysis[56] of system entropy has concluded that matter and energy alone, without the introduction of additional information, cannot lead to a decrease in entropy (and an increase in order.)

A cursory study of these life forms ... shows just how dissimilar they are.

When living creatures sustain all of the many processes of life, their bodies follow the information blueprint contained in their DNA. Part of the elegance of the design is its adaptability. However science seems to indicate that remarkable improvements in a design, which would create

[56] See Bibliography, McIntosh 2006.

an entirely new species, shouldn't happen suddenly. (For a system to produce useful work, its energy must be directed.) This would be tantamount to the random motion of water molecules in a bathtub suddenly aligning so that they all jumped straight up into the air, and came crashing back down again; or if half of them froze and the other half boiled away. These things are mathematically possible, but not observed in Nature. When they are, most would be inclined to call them a miracle[57]. Nevertheless, this is the difficulty faced by Naturalists. The fossil record shows gradual change within a particular body plan, but also the unexplainable appearance of entirely new and marvelous body plans.[58] The amount of new information contained in the definition of a new body plan seems to be too much to attribute to evolutionary processes. For a new species to suddenly appear, a staggering amount of information has to be introduced by an external agent (e.g. God) into the creature's DNA. Many of us would be compelled to call the sudden appearance of an entirely new creature a "miracle."

But what if life has had all along the innate ability to spontaneously evolve to higher life forms? It seems that this doesn't quite resolve the issue either. It turns out that earlier life forms were indeed simpler. We still must explain the motion from the simple to the complex – and the introduction of remarkable infusion of order and information into a system. If these were massive random changes to the DNA, then we would see the appearance of more mistakes than we would see of well formed creatures. Where are the overwhelming populations of misfits in the

---

[57] Especially if you were a runaway Jewish slave escaping from Pharaoh's army in Egypt across the Red Sea, and the timing of the event was perfect to suit your need. It would be hard to NOT call the parting of the Red Sea a miracle.

[58] Evolutionist J. Gould explains "a species does not arise gradually by the steady transformation of its ancestors; it appears all at once and 'fully formed.'" (Gould 1977) He theorizes that this can be explained by a process he calls "punctuated equilibrium."

fossil record? If only well formed creatures suddenly appear due to some undiscovered innate mechanism, then one has to answer “where did this innate information come from?”

4.3.15.2 The Origin of the First Life

The classic theory of evolution teaches that life began with “simple” single-celled life forms, but science has found that even the simplest of life forms are incredibly complex. This doesn’t mean that life didn’t begin with simple life forms, but that it is difficult to assume that such a life form could be formed entirely by natural causes. Many people, including agnostics, believe that life must have been “seeded” onto planet Earth by an external agent. To some this implies there must be a god. To others, this implies there must be aliens living in other solar systems who are very technically advanced. In either case, one is left asking “where did the alien(s) come from?” Certainly any physical being would have all of the same problems with origins that we would have. A being that lived beyond this physical realm however would not suffer the same constraints.

... some external agent must be responsible for these sudden appearances of new species that are fully formed.

4.3.15.3 Systems of Systems

The complexity at issue goes far beyond the complexity of a single species. Each life form (even bacteria) exhibits astronomical complexity.

When one considers the fact that these systems play a role in a larger ecosystem, the interrelationship and interdependencies formed between these systems of systems boggles the mind. To think of the cooperative role of producers, consumers, and decomposers; the "just right" proportion of sunlight, the size of the moon in relation to the Earth, and the amount and proportion of atmospheric gases; it seems incredible to think any life at all would be present much less an ecosystem. For a new species to "appear" and survive for millions of years requires everything in its environment to be "just right" for survival.

4.3.16 Can Everything be Explained Naturally?

Many things can be explained naturally, but not everything. When the evidence points to something unnatural happening, it seems fair to invoke a supernatural explanation.

Many things can be explained naturally, but not everything.

Some go to the extreme to believe that God brilliantly planned for life to evolve and that everything came about naturally after He set the Universe in motion. I have difficulty with this position as well because I believe that man is unique in that God made him in His own image and breathed the breath of (eternal) life into him. I also have difficulty with the thought that God would completely abandon His role in the development of the species, and rely instead on random mutation to generate creative ideas rather than employ His own. This isn't to say that adaptation doesn't occur, but that I believe evolution is inadequate for the job. God appears to have implemented entirely new body plans at specific points in Earth history as He saw fit. Evolution is useful to "tweak" a design and optimize it for a locale, but it just doesn't have the problem solving capability to develop solutions to the level observed in the fossil record.

4.3.16.1 Is evolution in the Bible?

The Bible does describe evolution and speciation.

The Bible describes God speaking things into existence. He not only said "light be" and "light was," but also "let the water teem with living creatures" and "let the land produce living creatures according to their kinds." The Bible records distinct moments in time when God intervened with any natural order to cause specific events to occur. Animals it seems were free to develop variety within their "kind."

The Bible describes some amount of evolution in plant life. Genesis 2:5 describes the timing of the creation of Adam—that he was formed before cultivatable field plants had "*sprung up*."[59] We know that the modern cultivatable plants such as wheat and corn are relatively modern inventions—coaxed by farmers for generations into what we have today. What did the first such plants look like, and when did they appear? These words imply to me that Adam was made at a time when certain primitive plants existed, and of course the specialized plants in the Garden of Eden, but not the cultivatable crop plants. By the time of the fall,

---

[59] At least they had not "sprung up" in the area where Adam was living.

cultivatable field plants had evolved.[60] The timing for this is impeccable because Adam needed a food source outside the Garden of Eden after the fall. Not only would Adam cultivate such crops, but also his descendants as they spread out from the central location (in response to their commission).

There is also some evidence of speciation among humans in the Bible. Genesis 6:4 says that there were "giants (Nephilim) in the land." This people group possessed extraordinary ability compared to normal humans. They were later destroyed in the flood during Noah's time.

Why would God make species of plants and animals that adapt? It's just a matter of good engineering! Engineers know that it is always desirable to design flexibility into the product. In microprocessor based products, it's common today to accomplish this largely though software upgrades. God designed a system using a different technique that supports variety. The variety not only makes species more interesting, it also maximizes the probability for successful survival of the species. In addition to designing-in adaptability, God shows His engineering prowess by designing systems that are self healing, self replicating, and part of a complete ecosystem that is self optimizing. These systems of systems go well beyond mans' ability to manage complexity and manipulate matter.

"Good engineering" involves not only "good design" but "good testing" as well. One could take the view that God tested each design (over long periods of time) before using it on more important species. It might seem ridiculous that God, (being who He is) should have to test anything. After all, if God is omniscient, He would certainly know what a design is capable of accomplishing. Engineers, however,

[60] "Evolved" in this case is used to mean "developed" as a result of the word spoken by God in Genesis 1 "Let the land bring forth vegetation."

know that tests serve multiple purposes. Tests not only prove the goodness of the design, they can be an important factor in customer acceptance. He (in a way that only He could enjoy) created plants, animals, and ultimately humans—all of whom were living "customers" for His work. When God pronounced everything to be "good" numerous times during the creation week, He was pronouncing the design to be good. Not only did all of the designs work, He proved that they work. He made a complex ecosystem with compatible "producers" and "consumers;" herbivores and carnivores. He made a comprehensive food supply, and a proven habitable environment before ever introducing His most demanding customer: man.

Could God have used evolution to make everything? The answer of course is "no." By definition,[61] evolution only attempts to understand how life forms change over time. It doesn't attempt to describe how life started in the first place. It also doesn't attempt to describe the origin of space and time.

4.3.17 Was it necessary for there to be a God in order for the universe to form?

This is a tough question which has become a matter of faith for many people. Another way to ask the question is if the finely tuned universe, and the complexity we see in life itself could have occurred as a result of some natural process. Random events (given enough time) can create complex results. Nature doesn't necessarily use random events for all of its processes. Some events which may appear to be random are actually rather limited in scope, methodic, and somewhat structured. The challenge a naturalist faces is to explain how <u>everything</u> could be explained naturally. I think that's a pretty tall order. There

---

[61] See the glossary at the end of the book.

are also negative consequences to this view. If God didn't somehow equip man with a heightened sense of right and wrong, then our conscience—something that distinguishes man from animal—must be dismissed as an evolutionary curiosity with no real basis in absolute truth. Another challenge for the naturalist is to consistently ignore God. The Bible is filled with stories of how God has reached out to man numerous times throughout history (e.g. Abraham and his journey, Moses and the burning bush, Peter and his catch of fish, Paul on the road to Damascus). Can I in good conscience say God doesn't exist? My faith won't let me.

Evolution doesn't attempt to describe how life started in the first place.

5 When did we get here?

Sections 4.3.7 and 4.3.12 described the history of the Earth in what the Bible calls "Day 2" and "Day 6." Science calls these same periods the "Hadean Eon" and the "Phanerozoic Eon" respectively. The physical evidence suggests that the Earth is approximately 4.5 billion years old. In contrast, Homo Sapian Sapian's presence on the Earth has only been for 150 thousand years. The earlier species called "Homo Sapian" is said to have appeared 300,000 to 500,000 years ago. The species called "Homo Habilis" is said to have appeared 1.8 million years ago. I guess the better question is "When did God make Adam?" and "Did God make Adam to be one of the older species?" The other species could have simply died out or been destroyed by Noah's flood—leaving Noah's family alone as our ancestors. Or on the other hand, did God make (or allow) other creatures that look like man to appear (perhaps in order to prove out the design), but not make Adam (the one into whom he breathed the breath of life) until some recent date. To try and find answers to these questions, we need to turn to the Bible for additional clues and compare this to dates provided in science.

5.1 What about the evidence of early man?

5.1.1 Timeline

The Bible doesn't really provide a solid timeline for man's creation.

Some have attempted to use the genealogy of Adam to compute a timeline, but the genealogies are incomplete. The genealogies list notable individuals but not every individual. This provides enough information to estimate a lower bound[62] but not necessarily a useful time frame.

I'd like to suggest there is another approach that can be taken—to merge Biblical clues with scientific ones. The Bible says[63] that man was made on the sixth day, and before the cultivatable crops in the field sprung up.[64] Adam was what anthropologists would call a "gatherer."[65] As a result of the fall, Adam became a farmer.[66] We later read[67] where one of Adam's sons, Cain, became a farmer. We're

---

[62] Using this incomplete method, some have estimated a lower bound of 6,000 years.

[63] Genesis 2:5 says "and no shrub of the field had yet appeared on the earth and no plant of the field had yet sprung up, for the Lord God had not sent rain on the earth and there was no man to work the ground." (NIV)

[64] The Bible clearly describes plants forming across the Earth on Day 3, with improvements in the plants occurring on successive days. For the Bible to say here that there were no plants in the field because of lack of rain is an apparent contradiction that is resolved in the context of the larger storytelling. Genesis is also known as "The First Book of Moses." I believe Moses had these events described to him by the Lord—quite possibly with a vision. Before the Earth existed, he could have seen the location of the Earth and realized it was "void and without form." As the vision progressed, he could see it form, he could see the atmosphere form around the Earth, plants grow, the debris from the accretion disk cleared by the solar wind to reveal direct sunlight and light the moon. As the vision progresses, he finds himself on the Earth, and in a particular location. This location is an arid desert except for the garden planted by the Lord, which has abundant water in the form of several rivers and artesian wells. In the context of the seer of the vision, and of the story, this location has "no rainfall," but that isn't to say other areas on the planet don't receive rainfall. This location has "no shrubs," but that isn't to say shrubs didn't exist elsewhere on the planet. The storyteller has already explained this portion of the story. The point being made here is that there was no need to use the land to grow cultivatable crops before man was made. Man's food would be supplied by the trees in the Garden of Eden. Only after man was driven from the Garden did other sources become important.

[65] Genesis 1:29

[66] Genesis 3:19

[67] Genesis 4:2

not told what he farmed. Adam, and later his son Cain, became the first farmers. They had their work cut out for them. It is unlikely that they grew crops that resemble the crops commonly grown today. They also likely had to develop irrigation techniques (unless rainfall increased).

While grass itself has been around longer than grazing animals, scientists[68] find that domestication of nearly all of the major foodstuffs (wheat, rice, barley, corn, etc.) started almost 10,000 years ago and all from grasses! The earliest domesticated form of wheat is domesticated Emmer, its predecessor, wild Emmer, formed in the fertile crescent area of the Near East over 30,000 years ago. This is the very area believed to be home to the Garden of Eden, Noah's ark, and well known areas of ancient civilization. Wild Emmer is a natural hybrid of two other grasses, one of them is closely related to Wild Einkorn, and the other[69] hasn't been positively identified. Using the Biblical clue of "cultivatable," it would place the origin of Adam sometime before 30,000 years ago. This 30,000 year timeframe establishes a Biblical lower bound for the age of man. This lower bound agrees[70] with the statement by scientists which place the appearance of modern man (Homo Sapian Sapian) approximately 150,000 years ago.

So now the question to ask is "Was Adam a member of the most recent species or an earlier species?"

5.1.2 Species

Fossils are hard to find. This makes piecing together a useful collection very difficult.

---

[68] Damania et. al.; Nesbitt; and narrative provided at New Hall Mill.

[69] It is believed by many to be a goat grass.

[70] On a scale of tens of thousands of years rather than millions or billions of years.

Anthropologists have found numerous skeletal remains which are different than modern man. Some of these remains clearly indicate substantially different species living in different time periods. Because fossils are hard to find, the complete list is perhaps unknown.

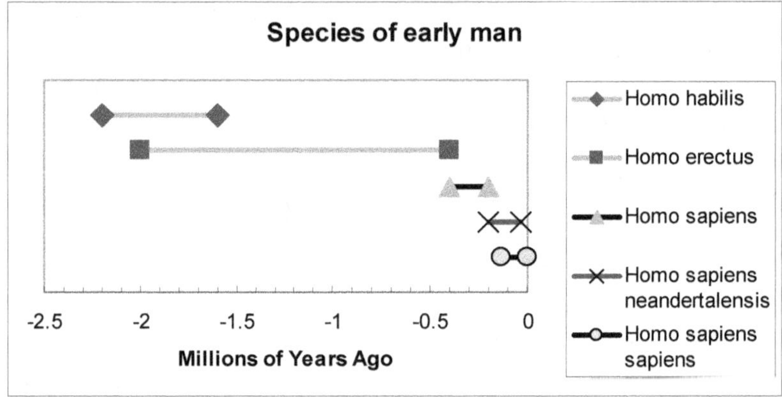

Figure 13—Species of early man[71] (WSU 2008)

God could have:

1.) Made Adam as the first of many species, and subsequent variations evolved from his linage, or
2.) Made many trial species prior to Adam, with Adam being the last in the series, or
3.) Made Adam somewhere between the first and the last in the series.

The important thing is that God made man. He made him for a purpose in accordance with a carefully laid plan. Just <u>when</u> He made man is a question that can remain unsettled. The fact <u>that</u> He made man is a core belief that you should resolve in your heart.

[71] Not shown on the timeline are the many parallel timelines of all of the other creatures that God had created before creating man. This would include the microevolution of apes and all other creatures.

The fact that He made man is a core belief...

5.1.2.1 Adam the "caveman"

On Day 6 God said "let the land bring forth creatures...." Man was made at the end of Day 6. What set him apart from the others who were also "out of the ground" is that he had been given a spirit.[72] He was spiritually aware. He had fellowship with God.[73]

In making Adam out of the ground, God may have made him "from scratch" or made him out of the ground by making him from a predecessor race which in turn was "out of the ground."

Early species prior to Homo Habilis had small brains[74] and apelike faces. These are largely considered animals—having the intelligence of apes.

Based on Adam's accomplishments listed in the Bible, it seems very unlikely that Adam could have been such a creature. Adam was said to have named all of the animals.[75] A creature with the intelligence of an ape wouldn't have the capacity for speech to perform such a feat.

The concept that man[76] had a rather sudden beginning fits rather well the story that God made the female shortly after

---

[72] Genesis 2:7

[73] Genesis 3:8 describes both the customary visit by "the voice of God" in the garden, as well as how the relationship was altered due to the fall of man.

[74] Some were one-third the size of Homo sapiens sapiens.

[75] Genesis 2:19

[76] Adam called his wife "Eve," but God called both of them "Adam." The term is used to denote "man-kind."

making the male, and the two of them were alone[77] in the garden that God planted. This doesn't require however that Adam be the first of all creatures to walk upright. Some of the species which apparently predated modern man seemed to enjoy quite a long run before eventually dying off. Adam could have been the first in one a subsequent species—which brings us to the next scenario.

5.1.2.2 Adam the "modern man"

A number of Bible expositors read the King James Version of the Bible[78] and cite where God told Adam to "replenish" the Earth. They conclude that there must have been a "pre-Adamic" race which was wiped out. God tells Adam (and Eve) to repopulate the Earth. The pre-Adamic race may have been either:

1. Creatures used to prove-out thc hominoid design and cultivate the ecosystem—yet likely enjoyed by God much as he enjoys the other animals[79], or
2. Individuals who knew God, rejected him, and became subject to God's judgment.[80]

If Adam was made as Homo Sapians Sapians, one has to ask "where did the Neanderthals come from?" The

---

[77] Genesis 2:18

[78] Genesis 1:28. The same word is also used in Genesis 9:1 when God tells Noah to "replenish" the Earth. The Hebrew word "אלמ" commonly means "fill."

[79] In addition to God's general pronouncement that the creation was "good," Job 40-41 appears to imply that God takes some delight in the animals He created..

[80] After all, God threatened on more than one occasion to wipe out civilization and start over (Gen 6:17, Deut 9:14, Matt 3:9, etc.) It's possible that our race is not the first, but only the latest. Much like the fallen Angels who have no plan of redemption, there is no requirement for God to be gracious toward a given group who acts wickedly. He may have given them life, but due to their wickedness, found it necessary to wipe them out and start over.

scientific evidence says that they were contemporaries of Homo Sapians Sapians—perhaps from a common ancestor.

There are still more issues to be discussed, and some of them are very sensitive. We might not have enough information to positively reach a conclusion, but it is a fascinating subject worth discussing.

Another issue to be addressed is the thought that all other species were "animals" and only Homo Sapian Sapian had God's breath of life. The question becomes "Did God make man initially from the ground, or did he take Homo Sapian Sapian (perhaps after many thousands of years of existence), and breathe the spiritual breath of life into him?" The Bible seems to indicate the former (that God made Adam out of the ground from scratch) but the fossil evidence shows similarities to other species.

If God were to breath life into an existent species and thus make Adam, one would have to take poetic license with the words "and God made man formed the man from the ground"—implying perhaps that Adam was "from the ground" because the creatures that God used were "out of the ground." The bigger problem with this position is that evolution by itself isn't considered sufficient to explain the presence of man. There appear to be numerous times in which God intervened in Earth history to create creatures with new body plans. It would be reasonable to expect that a similar intervention would occur here in the creation of Adam.

5.1.2.3 Adam's uniqueness.

There are clues in the Bible that we shouldn't overlook. God gave Adam his name "אדם." The name means "man" but it also means "ruddy." It's quite possible that Adam was different from the other species because he had skin (with a ruddy[81] skin tone), while the other species were more "apelike" (with fur). Unfortunately, we don't know much about the outward appearance of the other species, but if we discount all of the species that had apelike skeletons, it would imply that Adam had to be a species such as Homo Habilis or later.

Could other species have developed from Adam's line? The Bible says "yes!"

5.1.2.3.1 Biblical account of new species and races

Many who read the Bible have difficulty accounting for a species which is not modern man. After all, the Bible says that God created Adam and Eve. Where would other "races" or even "species" come from? We need to examine the Bible to find a possible answer.

> *When men began to increase in number on the earth and daughters were born to them, the sons of God saw that the daughters of men were beautiful, and they married any of them they chose. Then the Lord said, "My Spirit will not contend with man forever, for he is mortal; his days will be a hundred and twenty years."*
> *The Nephilim[82] were on the earth in those days—and also afterward[83]—when the sons of God went to the daughters of men and had children by them. They were the heroes of old, men of renown (Genesis 6:1-4).*

---

[81] I'm not trying to imply here that Adam had red hair and freckles. We humans call someone "red" who is exceptionally red. God may have named him that simply because he had a soil-colored complexion, which in comparison to the other creatures was "ruddy" (or reddish).
[82] The Hebrew word "Nephilim" is often interpreted to be "Giants."
[83] This passage is describing the time before the flood and saying that Giants existed before the flood, and also appeared afterward. This was particularly relevant to the Israelites as they faced some of their enemies.

This passage is describing a species of people that were offspring of Adam and Eve, yet larger. Where did they come from? Verses 1 and 2 describe how that the "Sons of God" intermarried with the "Daughters of Men." The meaning of this particular passage has troubled many readers of the Bible. Many experts suggest that these were the names of two groups of people. Commentators[84] explain that there were essentially two families in the ages before the flood: The descendants of Seth, and the descendants of Cain. Seth was considered a godly offspring, and Cain (going down in history as the first murderer) was considered ungodly. While Adam and Eve had many more children, there seems to be alignment with one camp or the other.[85]

Anthropologists describe how early man lived in tribal communities. Assuming practices at that time were similar to practices today; customs may have required that a wife be found amongst one's own tribe, or with a neighboring tribe with whom there were friendly relations.

The Biblical passage appears to describe a situation where there was a complete lapse of ethical norms. Men from the (supposedly) godly tribe were choosing wives from the tribe aligned against God. The consequences for this wholesale abandon were felt at a societal level. We also see the frustration level of the Lord rising because men resisted any attempt to follow the leading of His Spirit.[86] The ongoing moral decline of man sunk so low that it ultimately grieved God that He had made man in the first place.[87]

---

[84] Matthew Henry, Robert Jamieson, et. al.

[85] If these groups revered either God or man, then History has perhaps repeated itself time and again. Groups of men ("believers") revere God in contradistinction to those ("unbelievers") who revere man as the ultimate figurehead.

[86] To think that God's Spirit would contend with early man – Wow! God deals with men as He sees fit, according to His good pleasure.

[87] See Genesis 6:6.

The Nephilim were "men of renown." They were also contemporaries of early man. The Bible finds their population significant enough to mention. Interestingly enough, archeological finds indicate that Homo sapiens neandertalensis (Neanderthals) were also contemporaries of early man. While not any taller, they were all wider. Neanderthal skeletons indicate their bones were much stronger, were moved by massive muscles, and on average they had larger brains! It doesn't take much to imagine that such men would be called "men of renown." Could the Nephilim[88] be the Neanderthals?

Stories of their exploits would naturally circulate among the tribes. Cave art and other archeological evidence shows that stories of legendary exploits were commonly circulated among tribes in ancient times.[89]

Why the various species disappeared is somewhat of an archeological mystery, but not a mystery to the reader of the Bible. All of the people of the Earth (all of the descendants of Adam of Eve, every people group) had become so reprobate, and had such complete disregard for the Spirit of God, that God felt compelled to bring about a major extinction event to wipe them out.

> *The Lord saw how great man's wickedness on the earth had become, and that every inclination of the thoughts of his heart was only evil all the time. The Lord was grieved that he had made man on the earth, and his heart was filled with pain. So the Lord said, "I will wipe mankind, whom I have created, from the face of the earth ...for I am grieved that I have made them" (Genesis 6:5-7).*

---

[88] Perhaps in this case the term "giant" refers to mass or to width rather than height.
[89] The Cave of Lascaux.

There was one man however, Noah, who found favor with God, and listened to His voice.

> *...But Noah found favor in the eyes of the Lord...Noah was a righteous man, blameless among the people of his time, and he walked with God. Noah had three sons: Shem, Ham, and Japheth (Genesis 6:8-10).*

God instructed Noah to build an ark, and take his family (and sets of animals) on board. God sent the flood and it wiped out the others who were not aboard the ark. After the extinction event, Noah's family exited the ark and began to settle. The Bible describes the areas their offspring settled. Ham's descendants spread to the Southwest, Shem's descendants to the East, and Japheth's descendants to the North.

There are two competing anthropological theories to explain the origin of the races. One is that they evolved independently, and just happened to be very similar. (While this theory was popular years ago when racism was more prevalent, it has all of the problems of the theory of evolution compounded by the unlikely result of identical outcomes.[90]) The other theory is that some type of extinction event occurred which wiped out the other types of man, and that all of the races are descended from a single, small, people group.[91] This theory is not only more credible,[92] it fits the new physical evidence, and it agrees with the Biblical account.

---

[90] By this I mean that if the probability of the evolution of Homo Sapian Sapians is "H," and the number of races independently developing is "R," then the probability of their development is H^R. If "M" is the probability of surviving a global mass extinction event, and there are "N" such events, then the probability of such a population surviving to the present age is $H^R M^N$.

[91] Using the symbols developed above, this probability becomes $H^1 M^N$.

[92] Given the formulas developed above, the second theory becomes more likely by a factor of $(H^1 M^N) / (H^R M^N) = H^{(1-R.)}$

While the meaning of the word "race" continues to be debated, one might use it to attempt to establish obvious groupings to people groups based on their physical characteristics. Early work in this area by evolutionists established five such groups:

- Caucasoid
- Capoid
- Congoid
- Australoid
- Mongoloid

However, after a better understanding of the development of civilization and the migration of various people groups, most physical anthropologists today arrive at three basic groups:

- Negroid
- Caucasoid
- Mongoloid

This is remarkable because it honors the Biblical view. Ham's descendants settled to the Southwest of the Middle East, and probably extended to fill the continent of Africa. Shem's descendants settled to the East of the Middle East, and probably kept going to the whole of Southern Asia. Japheth's descendants settled to the North of the Middle East, and spread to Europe and apparently Northern Asia. The end result is that the continuum of "races" continue to this day organized by geographic distribution as described by the account of Noah's flood. All of the races are Homo Sapians Sapians—the lineage of Noah and his family. Other species which also descended from Adam did not survive.

Despite the controversy surrounding the subject, continued scientific research[93] are resulting in findings that agree with statements recorded long ago in the Bible. Since the Bible was penned long before the advent of modern science, its accuracy has to be considered stunning. The Bible presents its message in simple terms, and reads like a letter of a story told by someone who was there. The Storyteller[94] presented the basic facts, as well as material relevant to the relationship between God and man. It is this relationship after all, which gives purpose to man, and presumably motivated God to create all that we know.

5.2 *If God Made the Universe, Why Would He Take Such a Long Time in Doing So?*

If God is all powerful, why would He not make the universe in an instant? Why would He bother to make it over a long period of time? What would be the point?

There are those who would claim that "nothing lasts forever" (and by implication that "no one lasts forever"). There are those who would view "life" as a fortunate accident of nature. "Life" as we know it however, is more than just a single outcome of a single event. For life to be sustained over a long period of time may actually imply the oversight of a guiding hand at strategic points in history. The creation of the universe, and of life itself, testifies to God's eternal nature.

---

[93] New studies have proven that the various races (involved in the study) could have come from a common ancestor. Science has yet to prove that all races have come from a single ancestor, but research is underway at the time of this writing. This hypothetical ancestor has been dubbed "Mitocondrial Eve."

[94] The Lord gave Moses the story of creation. The Lord spans time and was personally involved in every event. The story is obviously from the Lord's perspective.

The creation of the universe testifies to God's eternal nature.

While we may view the "hills" as being old (because they are made of soil), the weathered rocks the soil came from are even older. While weathered rocks are old, the mountains that they came from are even older. The first mountains came from cooled lava. Lava was generated during the formation of the planet. The planet was formed from materials which were generated from the original stars. Space, time, light, and of course stars were formed on "Day 1" of creation. While much of the process leading to the formation of soil is "natural," the intervention by God at Day 1 which ultimately led to the formation of the soil was "supernatural." With suitable soil in place, God could intervene again to create plants to grow in the soil, and animals to eat the plants. He could have created all that we know, and bootstrapped the entire ecosystem in an instant, but He chose not to. The age of the "hills" testifies to the longevity of the One who set the processes in motion to form the hills.

The vastness of space gives proof to the power and magnificence of its Creator. The repeated intervention in space and time by the Creator speaks to His patience and permanence. It speaks to the fact that life as we know it today is not merely a momentary fluke that can be explained away as an expected statistical outcome. But rather, our presence here defies all odds. The presence of the universe itself, the careful balancing of the cosmic parameters, the complexity of life, the intelligence of man, and so many other unlikely outcomes multiplied together to produce life as we know it indicate the ongoing intervention of Someone who has stood by and intervened in the natural outcome to produce an outcome suited to His purposes.

The Bible says:

> *Great and marvelous are your deeds,*
> *Lord God Almighty.*
> *Just and true are your ways,*
> *King of the ages (Revelation 15:3).*

God deserves credit not just for the "gaps" in filling in where science can't explain an event with natural causes, but also for nature itself, and the natural processes it entails.

God deserves credit for nature itself.

The fossil record shows evidence of well designed species of plants and animals that could adapt to changing conditions in their environment, but also well designed plants and animals that couldn't adapt. These species would rather suddenly disappear by an "act of God," only to be replaced by a new species with another "act of God." Some of the improvements in plants and animals over the years can be explained by innate specialization—for which the designer should receive glory. But there are also "unexplainable" improvements in the designs of plants and animals over the years. There have been occasions where entirely new body plans have been introduced into nature, fully formed, and fully functional. This forms evidence of Someone living outside of the creation who is eternal, powerful, and intervenes as He sees fit. This not only leaves "believers" awestruck, but should also promote a sense of fear. The fossil record alone shows evidence that God exists, and that He has a long history of intervening[95] in the affairs on Earth, and that we should not think of ourselves as being potentially immune[96] from His intervention once again.

God cares, and because He cares He will not let civilization run amok.

God cares, and because He cares He will not let civilization run amok.

5.3 Conclusion

While we can't tell with certainty just how God made man, there should be no question as to God's commitment to mankind. Not only do we have His infallible word on the matter, we've seen Him humbling Himself to take on the form of man, to suffer and to die on our behalf. There should be no question that God is fully vested in the human project.

God is fully vested in the human project

---

[95] Genesis 6:7; Genesis 18,19; Deuteronomy 9:14

[96] After all, in Matthew 6:10, Jesus warned the Pharisees and Sadducees saying "… *do not think you can say to yourselves, 'We have Abraham as our father.' I tell you that out of these stones God can raise up children for Abraham.*"

6 Why are we here?

6.1 Does man have any intrinsic value?

Some philosophers and religions teach that man has no intrinsic value. They might teach that life is just an accident, or perhaps worse, a punishment of some kind. They might contend that individuals have no value, and that life is essentially meaningless. The Bible teaches however that there is one greater than the creation: its Creator. This individual had a plan which involved creating the universe and ultimately mankind. He made man "out of the ground"[97] yet also made him "in God's image" (Genesis 1:27). This not only makes man unique, it makes him valuable.[98] God made man on purpose and for a purpose.

God made man "out of the ground" yet also in His own image. This not only makes man unique, it makes him valuable.

[97] The Hebrew word for "man" is "Adam" which sounds like (and may be related to) the word the Hebrew word for "ground."

[98] See Genesis 9:6

6.2 What is "the meaning of life"?

So this then begs the larger question, "What is the meaning of life?" Is the universe (and ultimately mankind) a big accident? God, being a real individual, though being God and lacking nothing, still has desires. Understanding His desires is the key to understanding the reason for creation.

Understanding His desires is the key to understanding the reason for creation.

The Bible says that:

God desires godly offspring (Malachi 2:15),

and that we are His "field" or His "building" (in other words, His "project"). (See 1st Corinthians 3:9.) I believe He made the Universe, the Earth, and ultimately man as part of a project in which newly made individuals are (hopefully) "godly" individuals. He placed man in an environment in which he would have choices, and their true nature would be revealed. He chose, in this project, to make man "out of the ground." He didn't have to give man such humble origins. Since we are eternal beings, it's not just that He is seeking "godly offspring" for the here and now, but for the here and hereafter. He ultimately desires to bring us to a place where we are with Him throughout eternity.[99]

Scientists have long speculated: "What would the universe be like if it were different?" Some have envisioned that this universe perhaps formed out of a "mother universe." Some

---

[99] See the first part of John 17:24, the end of the book of Revelation.

speculate that there are perhaps other universes quite different from ours. The Bible indicates a similar thing: that a spiritual "universe" (i.e. "Heaven") exists in addition to the physical one that we know.[100]

When He made the Angels, He didn't make them quite as limited as man.[101] He made them "spirits," fully aware, and highly capable. They were given bodies made of "spirit" rather than "out of the ground." To the best of our knowledge, Angels don't have a plan for "salvation." The fallen Angels are fallen, and that's the way they are.

God desires godly offspring.

[100] Hebrews 11:3, and 2 Corinthians 12:2 offer examples. The Bible refers to three heavens: (1) the atmosphere, (2) the rest of the visible universe, and (3) God's home.
[101] Psalm 8:5

God felt compelled to demonstrate His love for man by becoming man.

7 How can I have a relationship with God?

God has existed throughout time, and even before time began. He is self sufficient, yet often times we see Him planning, building, and doing things. He's motivated to do these things. Why? We learn in 1 John 4:8 that "*God is Love.*" We also saw that in Malachi 2:15 that "*God desires godly offspring.*" God, being good, decided to promote a good thing by developing individuals who, like Himself, would be "godly."

We read in the Bible where things started out fine in the relationship between man and God, but eventually, over the course of time, sin developed in man's heart and he fell into rebellion against God. The trust relationship was broken. As if this weren't enough, history is repeated again and again as we each in turn deny God and do things which would break an already broken relationship. But there is good news. God is very wise and planned[102] for this contingency before He spoke the first words of creation. The godhead made a decision that when the time came, God the Son (Jesus) would pay the price to restore the relationship between God and man[103]. (After all, when one "forgives" another, doesn't he bear the hurt himself? He finds a way to absorb the cost without exacting it from the other party.)

When Adam and Eve fell from grace in the Garden of Eden[104] God left them with provisions, penalties, and a promise. The promise was that one of Eve's offspring

---

[102] After all, it was he who said (in Luke 14:27-33) how it is necessary to count the cost before undertaking a project.

[103] Jesus then became what is termed "the lamb slain from the foundation of the world" (see Revelation 13:8).

[104] Genesis 3.

would bruise (or crush) the evil. This was the first of many promises of One who would come. One of the most amazing stories in history is that God felt compelled to demonstrate His love for man by becoming man! God, being sinless, yet at the same time becoming man, created a situation where a man was sinless. He was exempt from the curse of Adam and Eve. He was uniquely qualified to break the curse for all. God the Son laid down His own life to pay the price demanded by God the Father. Christ's redemptive work on the Cross was the mechanism by which other men could be saved. With the agreed upon price paid in full, the God who is beyond space and time had the basis for a relationship with man (before and after the cross—throughout eternity).

7.1 How could God establish a relationship with you?

All sound relationships are built on trust and integrity. God of course gives people options. After all, love isn't love if it isn't voluntary. There will be someone or something that you love and value. What will it be? For someone who loves the truth, nothing but the truth will satisfy. Nothing but a relationship with the true and living God will settle the heart that remains hungry for the truth.

Many religions offer ways to elevate man to reach God. Christianity tells the story of God trying to reach man. Man has a long history of seeking his own path, and choosing his own "god(s)" – often in defiance of God's wishes and in defiance of the truth[105]. Nevertheless, God is longsuffering. His Spirit will draw His beloved. All who love the truth hear His voice[106] and listen to Him. Hearing the truth is certainly made easier when there is someone to explain it. But God will deal with people at multiple levels. He might

[105] See Joshua 24:15
[106] John 18:37

appeal to a person's conscience. He might speak to a person's heart. In the course of time, a person may realize that they want to live with a clean conscience and a pure heart. They may also find that they are unable to live the perfect life they aspire to. He has placed us in an environment where we can freely make choices. Then, given such authority, we find an occasion to use it selfishly. We sin, yet our mandate is to be godly. We are to think sinless thoughts, to love one another as He commanded,[107] to be perfect as He is perfect[108]—this is what He asks. How can we live up to sinless perfection? This is where we must rely on His mercy, forgiveness, and the price He paid. Only because of His love can we have a hope for a real love in eternal fellowship with Him.

While there is much more that could be said, I would like to encourage you to develop your relationship with God, and to seek out and embrace His truth. I would like to challenge you to call upon Him in prayer. I would also like to encourage you to follow up with your local area church and get answers to your questions. Please remember that there is nothing more important in life than your relationship with God. Your respect for truth and your relationship with the Lord will not only have consequences in this life, but in the life to come.

The Bible says:

> *To those who by persistence in doing good seek glory, honor and immortality, he will give eternal life.*
> *But for those who are self-seeking and who reject the truth and follow evil, there will be wrath and anger (Romans 2:7-8).*

---

[107] John 13:34.
[108] Mathew 5:48, Genesis 17:1.

There is nothing more important than your relationship with God.

Searching for the truth is simply a matter of using our hearts and heads to investigate a universe that God made discoverable.

8 Concluding Remarks

There are many, many points of agreement between the Bible and the findings of science. A few notable ones include:

- Space and time had a sudden beginning
- The heavens are being stretched out
- Plant life appeared first, then ocean life, then life on land
- Man appeared (was made) after all of the animals
- Man is made from materials that are "out of the ground"

Science and the Biblical creation account don't have to be at odds with one another. Theology can go places where science can't go, and science can offer intriguing and interesting truths meant to be discovered and appreciated. Where science can only postulate as to what may have precipitated the big bang, the Bible makes clear claims as to the cause.

Searching for the cause of the big bang remains one of the greatest quests of modern science. Even as scientists are unable to arrive at a satisfactory model for this momentous event, as believers we have already arrived at a satisfying cause for it all, and a deeper appreciation for the magnitude of His accomplishments.

Searching for the truth is simply a matter of using our hearts and heads to investigate a universe that God made discoverable. Truths are all around us: physical and spiritual.

Jesus said that

> *Everyone on the side of truth, listens to me (John 18:37).*

All things which are legitimately true must agree with one another.

Long periods of time transpired after the big bang until the first light emanated from our Sun. The Earth sat idle for long periods of time while it cooled off before the first life appeared. The continents rearranged themselves several times over as plants developed. God made many different sea, sky, and land animals over a long period of time, until quite recently his creative work culminated in the creation of man. Man enjoyed fellowship with his maker initially, but sin crept upon the scene and spoiled the relationship. At the right moment, a mere two thousand years ago, God stepped into time once again. His action on the cross served as a pivotal moment in Earth history. The cross is the mechanism through which God was able to restore His relationship with man. I'd like to encourage you to allow the truth to take preeminence in your life. Let it possess you, and find out what it is to have a relationship with our glorious Creator.

9 More Questions for Further Investigation

I find that sometimes people just aren't asking the right questions. Perhaps without realizing it, they've made a critical assumption that (mis)guides their judgment. Sometimes people with opposing viewpoints fail to communicate because they don't understand the underlying assumptions in play, or the subtle redefinition of terms that sometimes occur.

9.1 The Questions

1.) Do you "believe in God?" If so, what kind of god is your god? Is god "an individual" whom you can know and who can know you? Does god have likes and dislikes? Or rather is god in your view, if he exists at all, more like a force or property? Would god ever have such a thing as "a plan" or "a goal" that he is working toward?

2.) Can a "real scientist" believe in a personal God?

3.) What are the arguments for believing in an "old Earth" view, or for holding to the "young Earth" view?

4.) What do the events of Noah's flood have to do with the events of creation?

5.) On Day 1 we see that God said "let there be light." Who made the darkness? Why is there darkness at the start of Day 1? Gnostics believed that "matter" was intrinsically "evil." Who made matter?

6.) Compare the command given to Adam in Genesis 2:17 to the command Eve articulated in Genesis 3:3. Eve's account had more "information" in it than the original. Why did Eve say that they were not allowed to even touch the forbidden fruit? Where did she get this information? How did this contribute to her downfall?

7.) There are numerous views of the Creation account—including "Young Earth" and "Old Earth" viewpoints. Among Old Earth viewpoints, there exists "Progressive Creation" and "Progressive Evolution." There are also numerous naturalistic explanations including "classic Darwinism," and "punctuated equilibrium." In your opinion, which views have the best explanatory power? Why?

8.) What does the evidence of "The big bang" say about other religious views which claim that "god" is in nature? What does this say about religious views that describe a circle of life in which life goes on unabated in various forms from eternity past?

9.) For each of the 6 days of creation, the Bible says "*And there was evening, and there was morning.*" How does one explain "evening and morning" on days before there was a rotating Earth or an illuminated sun? On Day 3 plants are created. What sustained them until Day 4? Is this an argument for a 24-hour day?

10.) How do you explain the origin of all things?

11.) Having now described the framework you subscribe to, what are the implications regarding the responsibility of man? How should men live? Does he have a moral responsibility to a creator, or is he free to invent his own rules? What should those rules be? Why?

12.) Was there any death before the appearance of man? Was there any death before the fall of man in the Garden of Eden ?

13.) If the moon was formed on Day 3 and not revealed until Day 4, could there be meteorites that contain traces of ancient plant life?

14.) When were the stars made?

15.) What role did God the Father play in the creation?

16.) If God made the universe, then who made God?

17.) Why would God desire godly offspring?

9.2 The Author's Answers to the Questions

1.) Q: Do you believe in God?
A: This is a personal question, which if performed as a survey will produce the entire spectrum of answers. I believe that God is "knowable" and that He can (and does) know us; that God has a personality – that there are things he likes and dislikes; and that God has a plan for man (corporately and individually).

2.) Q: Can a real scientist believe in a personal God?
A: Some say that science in its purest form operates on theories, and is testable and falsifiable. Some people claim to believe only in things that can be proven (either mathematically or experimentally). By this question, some try to imply that unless they apply such a philosophy consistently to every aspect of their lives, they are not a true "scientist." It would be very unusual however for a person to apply such a philosophy consistently to every aspect of their lives. We all use unproven theories to fill the gaps where we don't understand. For example, very few people understand the latest theories on superconductivity and the models of how an electron travels through a wire, yet we all enjoy the benefits of electrical power. We flip a switch and the lights in the room come on. We don't have to know "how" it works to benefit from "what" it is. We might know "what" it does, but not "why." Why would a material be a resistor at one temperature and a superconductor at another? Would a person who claims to be a "true scientist" not use electricity because they have yet to devise an experiment to unravel the mystery of electron mobility? Such a person would have to withdraw from society altogether. We eat food that we don't entirely understand how it grows. We interact with other individuals, yet can't read their minds or prove what we believe they are thinking. The fact is that all individuals (including

scientists) will build cognitive models (theories) to supplement their understanding. They will rely on these models as a frame of reference from which to interpret the world. The fact is that the scientific method cannot be applied to certain areas that are considered "untestable." Proof of the existence of God is one of these areas. Believing that there is a God doesn't diminish the value of nature, but rather adds value. It gives nature a purpose. Concepts of "truth" and "beauty" take on a new meaning. If we define a "scientist" to be one who studies nature in an effort to understand how it works, then certainly a "true scientist" can also believe in God if he wishes. The rainbow can still be awe inspiring even if one understands that it is caused by sunlight refracting through water droplets suspended in the air. It is still remarkable and beautiful. To a scientist who is also a Bible student, it may go on to also serve as a symbol to remind one of Noah's flood, and of a promise from God.

The same argument can be used on those who profess to be "true believers." What do "people of faith" do in areas where the book they turn to as an authority is silent? Should one not "believe in germs" because the Bible is silent on the subject? If the believers have been taught well, they've been taught to promote the truth and to be respectful of discoveries which are established as fact.

3.) Q: What are the arguments for believing in an "old Earth"?
A: Entire books have been written on the "young Earth" and "old Earth" debate. I encourage you to seek them out for more details. Many who promote the young Earth viewpoint perhaps do so over concerns that the Genesis account of creation would otherwise be compromised. If evolution were to gain the upper hand, then perhaps the belief in a literal "Adam" and a literal "Eve" would also perish. Man's fall and redemption would be reduced to

fanciful tales. Those who study the geological record do find that there are periodic upheavals in various locations that make any type of geologic timeline difficult to construct. While it may be difficult, it doesn't make it impossible; neither does it mean that the planet is only 6,000 years old. For decades, considerable study has occurred of sites all over the world. The story the rocks tell us is amazing. Some of the oldest rocks indicate that the Earth is nearly as old as the universe.[109] If a person really loves the truth, then he or she has to let the truth take its course. Believers—especially religious leaders—should not fear the truth. I find that the evidence says that the universe is quite old. After reading this book, I hope that you find that an old Earth doesn't prevent God from creating a literal Adam and Eve.

4.) Q: What do the events of Noah's flood have to do with the events of creation?
A: There have been a number of major extinction events in the Earth's history. Noah's flood is significant in that it was a (near) extinction event for mankind. It probably had quite an effect on some of the terrain.

5.) Q: Who made the darkness?
A: In the Bible, God says "I form the light and create darkness…." (Isaiah 45:7) God made the energy and matter we find in our universe. I believe the "light" and "dark" described on each of the six days of creation refers to spiritual light. The absence of God's radiant presence is described as "darkness."

6.) Q: Why did Eve say that they were not allowed to even touch the forbidden fruit?
A: I just have to believe that Eve recounted what Adam told her, and that Adam added content to the Lord's command in an effort to protect her. His admonition to not even touch

---

[109] On the order of 13 billion years.

the forbidden fruit completely backfired when she examined the fruit and found it suitable. This called into question the validity of everything else Adam told her. Satan used this to his advantage. There is a moral in this story—that those who attempt to speak for God should be careful to not add to what He has said. It is important that society have experts who are proficient in religious studies, and who teach others, but it is also important that they not overstep their bounds—lest their limits be exposed and their teaching discredited.

7.) Q: Which views of the Creation account have the best explanatory power?
A: Like this first question in the series, if offered as a survey, this one could likely yield a spectrum of answers. For whatever it's worth my views have "evolved" over time. I currently favor an Old Earth Progressive Creationism view.[110] I used to favor a Young Earth view (because that is what I was taught) but found the argument given by many preachers to be theologically unacceptable. A Young Earth advocate might say that God made the universe 6,000 years ago, but made it appear to be millions of years old.[111] This is something that an *all-powerful* God could certainly do. But I believe a *just* God would not do. He would not create a façade. So while His power enables Him to do such a thing, His morality restrains Him. The better I come to know of His ways, the better I appreciate that there is no deception in His character whatsoever. He will hide (or obscure) things from us, but He will never lie to us. I therefore choose to honor the God of the ages who is able to perform all things in a true and an upright fashion. I find that Biblical teaching and scientific teachings can be aligned with each other.

---

[110] And thus the book so that I may share my teaching with others.
[111] Because for example, the light from the stars takes millions of years to travel here.

8.) Q: How can various religious views deal with the evidence of the big bang?
A: For many religions, the thought of a sudden beginning is quite complementary to their ideology. For others it is problematic. Often the real issue isn't often as much the origin of the universe as it is the origin of man. If God made man, then man is accountable to God. This is truly problematic for people with humanistic world views who wish to declare their independence from God.

9.) Q: How does one explain "evening and morning" on days before there was a rotating Earth or an illuminated sun?
A: The idea of there being a cycle of night and day before the apparent creation of the Sun or Earth is really quite a stumbling block for many. A 24-hour-day creationist would view these days as precise 24-hour periods. I contend that this is reading information into the text which doesn't exist. In a similar fashion, the creation of plants before the supposed creation of the Sun is a stumbling block for those who would attempt to use the same framework to establish an old Earth view. I contend that this too is a mistake in the interpretation of the text. The point of the book is to attribute the cycles of light and dark to the presence or absence of God Himself. The light producing mechanisms He established on Day 1 continue working through all of the successive days. Plants benefit from it beginning on Day 3, and humans on Day 6.

10.) Q: How do you explain the origin of all things?
A: We either have to believe the development of life was undirected or directed.

> i.) Both science and the Bible indicate it was directed.
>
> ii.) Could life have been internally directed to develop into increasingly complex forms?

We've found that this simply isn't the way it works. The DNA of primitive life was smaller and encoded simpler information. The original information, and any increase in complexity must be the result of information added from external sources.

iii.) Could gradual change be the primary mechanism for the development of new species?

Nature does allow for variety to develop within species. Nature will also eliminate certain members of the population. If these mechanisms were the sole explanation for all species, then the fossil record should show a continuous progression from one species to another. The absence of these transitional forms poses a significant problem for this particular view.

iv.) Could random mutation be the primary mechanism for the development of new species?

Mistakes are occasionally made in DNA sequences and birth defects develop. Could a random change result in an improvement? With many countless random changes, and all unviable changes resulting in death, improvements could in theory occur – but at great cost. Fortunately however, neither our own experience, nor the fossil record supports this view. If this were the mechanism, the fossil record (as well as our daily experience) should be replete with horrific mutants. The fact that each "kind" reproduces after its own "kind" (rather than mutants) results in each species being maintained.

v.) Could the development of life have been occasionally directed by some external agent to take on radically different forms, and in the interim allowed to undergo gradual change?

The fossil record does show the sudden appearance of new fully-formed body types. Over time each body type develops variety. The information content introduced with each fully-functional, new body-type is staggering. Many have concluded that this indicates the presence of an alien agent who has introduced information into life-forms and directed their development.

The author's view is that God is the agent that created all living things, as well as "nature" itself.

11.) Q: What are the implications regarding the responsibility of man?
A: God gave special attention to the creation of man. With regard to the law, we should recognize that God is a real individual and not just a "force." He has likes and dislikes. He offered a set of rules to Moses for societal conduct. These laws flow from God and provide grounds for all societal laws built on their principles.

One of the rules in the Law of Moses is to honor one's parents. With God being Adam's parent, it obligates all according to this line of reasoning to honor Him. We should bear in mind that there are different levels of quality attainable in a relationship. If one desires to have a close relationship with Him, it requires finding out the true desires of His heart, and doing all of the things that please Him.

12.) Q; Was there any death before the appearance of man or before the fall of man?
A: There are those who believe that there wasn't. I have to believe that all plants and animals were designed to have a limited lifespan. The universe itself has a limited lifespan. All physical things will eventually cease to function. This isn't something to worry about for those who are near to God. When God told Adam that he would die if he ate of the forbidden fruit, He was referring to spiritual death—separation from God. (This is something to worry about!)

I have to believe that even before the appearance of man, carnivores and scavengers ate meat, and that the meat came from dead animals. Think about a world in which life could reproduce but not die. What would it be like? It sounds like a bad science fiction / horror novel. Only the plants that had access to sunlight would be fed. Everything else would go hungry. It is the death of plants and animals that provides opportunities for higher life forms to manage an existence, and entire ecosystems to be developed. God made the ecosystem, and should receive glory for creating all of the creatures in it.

13.) Q: Could there be traces of ancient plant life in meteorites?
A: It's interesting to note that God didn't pronounce the end of day 2 as being "good." It may be that there was unfinished business such as the formation of the moon.
In theory, if a very large meteorite struck the Earth it would devastate the planet and scatter debris into space. If the collision happened after primitive plants were formed, we might one day find evidence of ancient plant life on the moon, in meteorites, or on other nearby planets.

14.) Q: When were the stars made?
A: Science teaches that shortly after the Big bang the universe became transparent, hydrogen molecules formed

and coalesced into primitive stars. These early stars existed 13.3 billion years ago. Since then, stellar nurseries have been continuously forming new stars. Our Sun began its main sequence 4.57 billion years ago.

This book teaches that many stars, as well as the mechanism to produce stars, were all made on Day 1 when God said "let there be light." The stars however were not visible to an observer on Earth until the Sun began its main sequence on Day 4 and blew away dust in the accretion disk.

15.) Q: What role did God the Father play in the creation?
A: My view is that while all of the members of the Godhead played an active role in the creation, they each played different parts. I view the Father as the one who is primarily responsible for planning. He is however, eternal and self-existent. He is the source of all things. He is worthy to be feared. He is the mathematical singularity which many scientists say must exist to explain the formation of the universe. Living beyond space and time, unconstrained by the laws of physics, He is impossible for us to know in the physical sense, so He "begat" a Son and sent Him into the world to explain the Father. Jesus encourages those who have been "born from above" to pray (directly) to the Father. For, while we cannot know Him in the physical sense, we can know Him in the spirit.

16.) Q: If God made the universe, then who made God?
A: This is perhaps beyond our comprehension and experience, but material things which exist in this time-space continuum have a beginning and an end. Since God is not made out of matter, and exists beyond our comprehension of time and space, He is not subject to the same limitations as we. He doesn't have a beginning or end. He doesn't need a "creator"—having always existed.

17.) Q: Why would God desire godly offspring?
A: This question speaks to the very nature of God. I find the fact that God would actually want something to be a thought worth pondering. What would you give to the God who has everything? Do I have something I can give Him to satisfy His desire? (He of course wants us to live godly lives and be the godly offspring.)

The fact that He desires something also says that He has a personality. He is more than just a "system" which emanates and ultimately judges life. All life comes from God, and ultimately, all life must answer to God.

Why would He desire offspring at all? Some might say that the world is so messed up, who could bring offspring into such a world? We need to remember that before the fall of man, the creation was pronounced "good." Even after fall, man received promises from the Lord to give us assurance. No one is able to snatch us from His hand.

While God is light, and in Him is no darkness at all,[112] His light does cast a shadow and we can see a distinction between what He is and what He isn't. We can see a difference between what He subscribes to and what He doesn't. We see early on the formation of two camps within the human race.[113] One camp aligned with "Abel" and called themselves the "sons of God." Another camp aligned with "Cain," rebelled against God, and called themselves the sons (and daughters) of man. This selection is made repeatedly throughout history as generations choose how they will live. Do they live for themselves, or do they live for God? Jesus taught that those who seek to find their lives will lose it, but those who give their lives away will find it.

[112] 1 John 1:5
[113] Genesis 6:1

The happiest people are the ones who have learned to live for something larger than themselves—the ones who validate their existence by loving and helping others.

So, did God create man out of a need He has to help others? I say "no." He is self-sufficient and has need of nothing. Rather, He created man out of an overflowing abundance of love. After all, the Bible says that "God is love."[114] The "offspring" He created became the objects of His affection. This same love however wants only the best for His children. He is rightfully upset when any of them act in an unloving fashion toward one another.[115] He will judge sin. He will judge the fallen angels. He will judge sinful man.

In order to be truly "godly," we (His offspring) must have (or develop) godly character. This means that we must:

- Have an overflowing abundance of love.
- Choose what is right and eschew evil—even at great personal expense.

Although we live in a "fallen" world, we were born into a universe in which we would inescapably have certain needs. Our bodies are made of matter, and all matter will eventually follow the course of the universe.[116] Given then that we have a finite lifespan (even if we didn't live in a fallen world), we were born into a world in which we have needs. We must call on God for His rescue. Given then that we were made some distance away from God, we are in a position to see His example and to see alternatives. Which will we choose? We will choose what we want to choose based on what we love. Which do we love? Do we love

---

[114] See 1 John 4:8.

[115] Is this unreasonable? Don't we as parents get upset when our children act in an unloving manner?

[116] Many billions of years from now, the universe is expected to either wind down or rip apart. In either case, it is the "end of physical life" for all creatures throughout the universe.

others, or do we love ourselves preeminently? Are we "givers" or "takers"? If we love others, we will also love "the law" in the sense that we will love what is fair and just. We will hate injustice. If we love others above ourselves, we will also be willing to make a sacrifice in order to help them. Some of us may be called upon to make the ultimate sacrifice. (How could God do anything less than offer Himself as the ultimate example through the life and death of Jesus?)

The environment in which we live is the ultimate proving ground for "godliness." We find other people around us who have needs. Do we take advantage of them, or do we help them? Is there a better environment than this one in which God could develop and prove our character? Is there a better environment than this one in which to love God, love our fellow man, and demonstrate it by the life we live?

All life comes from God, and ultimately, all life must answer to God.

I find that Biblical teaching and scientific teachings can be aligned with each other.

10 Glossary

bootstrap, to powerup a system – going from a dead lifeless state to a fully animated state.

engineer, One who has knowledge in one or more fields of science, and seeks to apply his understanding of scientific principles to develop products for the betterment of mankind.

evolution, The study of how life changes after it originates.[117]

fermion, A particle, such as an electron, proton, or neutron, having half-integral spin and obeying statistical rules requiring that not more than one in a set of identical particles may occupy a particular quantum state. (Dictionary 2004)

miracle, Although all natural processes are attributable to God, an event is considered a "miracle" when God intervenes to alter the natural order of events (which he has otherwise previously set into motion).

physical death, To be separated from one's body due to bodily malfunction.

physical life, to be physically animated.

protosun, (*astronomy*) The condensation of material that lay at the center of the solar nebula and accreted material from it to form the sun. (Answers.com 2003)

---

[117] Stephen J. Gould as quoted in Witham 2002.

scientist, One who seeks to understand the workings of nature, and who has attained expert knowledge in one or more areas of science.

science,

1.) A branch of knowledge or study dealing with a body of facts or truths systematically arranged and showing the operation of general laws: *the mathematical sciences.* (Dictionary 2006)
2.) The investigation of the natural world through the use of observation, experimentation, and logical argument. (Wells 2005)

spiritual death, To be separated from God.

spiritual life, To be connected to, or have an upstanding relationship with God.

terraform, To alter the environment of (a celestial body) in order to make capable of supporting terrestrial life forms. (Random House 2009)

11 More Background: Methods of interpretation

A number of interpretations endeavor to explain the evidence:

- The classic Darwinian view attributes everything to natural causes with no consideration for the Biblical view whatsoever.
- Certain old-Earth creationists introduce an element of Godly influence to say that God used evolution to create life.
- Other old-Earth creationists introduce considerably more Godly influence to say that God stepped in at appropriate moments to order the development of the universe.
- Still others believe in a young-Earth creation, and that God created the universe in six 24-hour days about 6,000 years ago.

11.1 Interpretation of the evidence

It is natural for us to interpret what we see within the framework of what we know. This isn't a bad thing. It allows us to be very proficient at interpreting our surroundings. Science leverages this human ability in a formal way to identify a concept as a "theory." A theory may have a testable "hypothesis" which serves to confirm or deny the theory. A theory is valuable if it fits all of the evidence, and particularly useful if it can then predict the existence of something no one has ever seen. Once a theory is validated by reproducible tests, it is usually promoted to be considered a scientific "fact" within the community. Many theories remain just that because they lack evidence to substantiate them. This doesn't prevent certain zealous proponents of the theory from embracing them as fact, but technically they remain theories none the less. Similarly, theologians recognize that different people will operate under different belief systems. They would call a belief system a "world-view."

11.2 The Biblical creation account

Christianity teaches that God is rational, that He made the universe, and that His creation can be rationally understood. Early man began to understand the world in which we live and make use of it to better their lives.

Christianity teaches that God is rational and that His creation can be rationally understood.

Modern believers began to understand nature as something that was predictable. Newton, Pascal, and numerous other scientists who had deep religious convictions began to see patterns in nature, and to understand that every action had an equal and opposite reaction; that processes had reproducible outcomes; and that theories could be proven by carefully designed experiments. The efforts of these believers led to the dawn of the scientific era. The scientific era led to the industrial revolution, and the industrial revolution led to this modern age.

11.3 The Scientific approach

Science is a study of nature. Modern science presupposes that the subject under study can be rationally understood, and once understood, modeled. The strength of science is that once properly modeled, it can accurately predict the outcome of an event, and the results are ALWAYS reproducible.

The scientific method is well known: to make a hypothesis and then design and perform an experiment that will confirm (or deny) it.[118]

11.4 Atheism

Atheism begins with the belief that there is no God, and therefore that all that there is can be explained naturally.

Which world-view does the data support?

It is natural for atheists[119] to turn to science for answers. This however doesn't make all scientists atheists. Atheists can be expected to rely (religiously) on science because it fits nicely with their world-view. The question becomes "which world-view does the data support?" Good science, when properly done, doesn't necessarily lead to the conclusions that the atheists are hoping for.

11.5 The Clash of Interpretive Frameworks

Adherents on both sides tend to interpret the findings through their respective framework and accept or reject conclusions according to how well it fits the framework which they have accepted as true. As a result those who seek to explain everything by natural processes have difficulty writing an equation that says "...and then a miracle happens at this point." Those who believe that God exists and played an important role in the creation of all things have difficulty with those who refuse to entertain the very idea of a god.

---

[118] Sometimes it is easier to prove something isn't true than to prove that it is.
[119] And specialized forms of atheism such as Marxism.

The debate of creation vs. evolution in the public schools has inescapable religious overtones. The discussion is not merely over how we got here, but ultimately over the existence of God, and man's accountability to Him.

This debate leaves the believer in a situation where his beliefs are challenged. Should he trust emphatically what "the preacher" says (someone who is probably not a credible authority on science); or should he trust what "the professor" says (one who is probably not interested in having a religious framework imposed upon his work).

11.5.1 Good Science

When "good science" is practiced, the science is allowed to run its course. If the results are inconclusive, then that is the result that is communicated. When good science is practiced, results are not overstated. Analysis of the data can be described as fitting the model, or the expected results, but if a phenomenon is untestable or unobservable, then good scientific practice will confess "science can't explain it" (and perhaps positing a theory nonetheless).

When good science is practiced, the science is allowed to run its course.

11.5.2 The Way of Building Knowledge

In the scientific community, there is always an interest in advancing the state of the art. Improvements are often evolutionary rather than revolutionary. Practioners of the art often research the current findings, then advance it by developing a hypothesis, and performing experiments to prove or disprove the theory.

In the religious community, learning occurs differently. It usually occurs with sudden revolutionary revelations to an individual. The revelations can be quite revolutionary, and widely debated for centuries. Believers will grasp basic truths, and over time, progress to grasp more advanced teachings. Believers will learn from teachers, and might call on God for wisdom and guidance, and occasionally God will perform a miracle in order to validate His teaching.[120] (Compare this to science, where anyone can run an experiment and reproduce the findings.)

To have and operate under a belief system is natural, and expected. It's the way we were built. We sometimes need to be aware however that what is taught as "fact" is sometimes an overstatement of the truth.

11.5.3 Good Biblical Exposition

Good Biblical exposition will explain the Biblical text, and be vocal where the scripture is vocal, and silent where the scripture is silent. To add information as "fact" which isn't really borne out by the text, is the same mistake a scientist might make in adding unwarranted digits of precision to a numerical value. Sometimes it is necessary to re-examine the original text to see if differing shades of meaning have been inadvertently introduced in the translation.

[120] This is not to say that experiments have never been done by believers. A notable example is found in Judges 6:37-40 where Gideon experimented with a wool fleece. Another example might be found with the priestly use of the Urim and Thummim and the use of lots.

12 Bibliography

Astronomy Magazine, "50 Greatest Mysteries of the Universe," Kalmbach Publishing Company, (Special Edition) 2007.

Damania, et. al., editors, The Harlan Symposium, The Origins of Agriculture and Crop Domestication, "Part 1. Centers of Origins of Crop Plants and Agriculture," ICARDA, International Center for Agricultural Research in the Dry Areas © 1998, accessed 23 August 2008, http://www.ipgri.cgiar.org/Publications/HTMLPublications/47/index.htm .

Excoffier, L., and A. Langaney, "Origin and Differentiation of Human Mitochondiral DNA, *American Journal of Human Genetics*, 44:73-85, 1989.

France, "The Cave of Lascaux," Ministry of Culture and Communication. Accessed 28 Aug 2008, http://www.culture.gouv.fr/culture/arcnat/lascaux/en/ .

fermion. The American Heritage® Dictionary of the English Language, Fourth Edition. Houghton Mifflin Company, 2004. *Answers.com.* Accessed 19 Jan. 2009. http://www.answers.com/topic/fermion

Gould, J. Natural History, vol. 86, no. 5, ©1997.

Hanegraaff, Hank. Fatal Flaws: *What Evolutionists Don't Want You To Know,* W Publishing Group, Nashville, Tennessee 37214, © 2003.

Henry, Matthew. "Commentary on Genesis 1." Matthew Henry Commentary on the Whole Bible. Blue Letter Bible. 01 Mar 1996. 24 Aug 2008.

<http://www.blueletterbible.org/Comm/mhc/Gen/Gen001.html>.

Jamieson, Robert; A.R. Fausset; and David Brown. "The First Book of Moses, Called Genesis." Commentary Critical and Explanatory on the Whole Bible. Blue Letter Bible. 19 Feb 2000. 24 Aug 2008. <http://www.blueletterbible.org/Comm/jfb/Gen/Gen006.html>.

Jewitt, David. "Kuiper Belt," University Of Hawaii, Institute for Astronomy, 13 January 2008, <http://www.ifa.hawaii.edu/faculty/jewitt/kb.html>.

Johnson, Ashley S. "Daughters of Men," *Condensed Biblical Cyclopedia*, Blue Letter Bible, 1 Jul 2002, 12 Jan 2008. <http://blueletterbible.org/study/cbc/cbc09.html> .

McIntosh, A. C. "Functional information and entropy in living systems" in Design and Nature III: Comparing Design in Nature with Science and Engineering, pp. 115-126, Wessex Institute of Technology, WIT Transactions on Ecology and the Environment, Vol 87, WIT Press, Southampton UK, © 2006

National Aeronautics and Space Administration. "Oort Cloud," 13 January 2008. http://solarsystem.nasa.gov/planets/profile.cfm?Object=OortCloud.

Nesbitt, Mark. "Wheat evolution: integrating archaeological and biological evidence." In Caligari, P.D.S. & Brandham, P.E. (eds.), *Wheat taxonomy: the legacy of John Percival*, 37-59. London: Linnean Society, Linnean Special Issue 3, © 2001, accessed 21 August 2008 at http://www.kew.org/scihort/ecbot/papers/nesbitt2001wheat.pdf .

New Hall Mill. "Evolution of Wheat," 21 August 2008, http://www.newhallmill.org.uk/wht-evol.htm .

Penn State. "First Land Plants And Fungi Changed Earth's Climate, Paving The Way For Explosive Evolution Of Land Animals, New Gene Study Suggests." ScienceDaily 10 August 2001. 6 January 2008 <http://www.sciencedaily.com /releases/2001/08/010810070021.htm>.

protosun. Answers.com. *McGraw-Hill Dictionary of Scientific and Technical Terms*, McGraw-Hill Companies, Inc., 2003. accessed 18 January 2009 at <http://www.answers.com/topic/protosun>.

science. Dictionary.com. *Random House Unabridged Dictionary (v 1.1).* Random House, Inc., © 2006, accessed 24 May 2008 at <Dictionary.com http://dictionary.reference.com/browse/science>.

Stevenson, John. OneLife, ©1996-2006, 25 January 2007 accessed 8 October 2008 at http://www.onelife.com .

Strobel, Lee. The Case for a Creator: *A Journalist Investigates Scientific Evidence That Points Toward God*, Zondervan, Grand Rapids, MI, 49530, ©2004.

terraform. *Dictionary.com Unabridged (v 1.1)*. Random House, Inc. 18 Jan. 2009. <Dictionary.com http://dictionary.reference.com/browse/terraform>.

University Of Utah (2005, February 28.) The Oldest Homo Sapiens: Fossils Push Human Emergence Back To 195,000 Years Ago. *ScienceDaily*. Retrieved January

12, 2008, from http://www.sciencedaily.com /releases/2005/02/050223122209.htm.

Witham, Larry, Where Darwin Meets the Bible: *Creationists and Evolutionists in America*, Oxford University Press, New York, NY, 10016, © 2002.

Washington Statue University. *Hominoid Species Timeline,* 12 Jan 2008, <http://www.wsu.edu:8001/vwsu/ gened/learn-modules/top_longfor/timeline/ timeline.html>.

Wells, Jonathan. "Definitions of Science in State Standards," Discovery Institute, 10 November 2005, accessed at http://www.discovery.org/scripts/ viewDB/filesDB-download.php?id=333 on 24 May 2008.

Washington State University, "*Hominoid Species Timeline,*" accessed at http://www.wsu.edu:8001/ vwsu/gened/learn-modules/top_longfor/timeline/ timeline.html on 19 October 2008.

13 Index

www.ingramcontent.com/pod-product-compliance
Lightning Source LLC
LaVergne TN
LVHW020632100826
845148LV00012B/2152

* 9 7 8 0 9 8 2 2 7 5 1 0 8 *